The 1000 most important questions you will ever ask yourself

The 1000 most important questions you will ever ask yourself

That make life work for you

Alyss Thomas

First published 2005
This edition published 2011

Exisle Publishing Limited
'Moonrising', Narone Creek Road, Wollombi, NSW 2325, Australia
P.O. Box 60-490, Titirangi, Auckland 0642, New Zealand
www.exislepublishing.com

Copyright © 2005 & 2011 in text: Alyss Thomas
Alyss Thomas asserts the moral right to be identified as the author of this work.

All rights reserved. Except for short extracts for the purpose of review, no part of this book may be reproduced, stored in a retrieval system or transmitted in any form or by any means, whether electronic, mechanical, photocopying, recording or otherwise, without prior written permission from the publisher.

National Library of Australia Cataloguing-in-Publication Data:
Thomas, Alyss, 1957-
The 1000 most important questions you will ever ask yourself : that make life work for you / Alyss Thomas.
2nd ed.
9781921497322 (pbk.)
Includes bibliographical references.
Success.
Self-esteem in young adults.
Self-acceptance.
Conduct of life.
158.10835

Cover design by Jef Tan
Text design and production by BookNZ
Printed in Singapore by KHL Printing Co Pte Ltd

This book uses paper sourced under ISO 14001 guidelines from well-managed forests and other controlled sources.

10 9 8 7 6 5 4 3 2 1

For Matthew
19.4.82 – 17.1.02

ACKNOWLEDGEMENTS

I am grateful to all my teachers, past and present, who have taught me more than I can remember. Thanks also to Gareth and Benny for imagining and bringing this project to life.

contents

Introduction	13
A new oracle of change	15
Why you don't need a fix	15
The trap of negativity, complaining, hopelessness, low self-esteem, guilt and self-blame	16
Why should I?	16
Thinking	17
Do I deserve this?	18
Denial and excuses	18
How this book works	19
Chapter 1 Ask Yourself	21
What do I really want?	22
The life questions	26
Action	27
What do *you* want to get sorted?	27
Action Planner	28
Confidence and self-esteem	34
Rate your self-esteem	35
Seven exercises for developing self-esteem	39
Self-confidence work-out	40
Plan for success	43
Thirteen successful outcomes	43
Self-sabotage	46
How much do you sabotage yourself?	49
Chapter 2 Choose Your Values	57
What are your values?	58
Decide on your values	59
The values list	61
The values work-out	69
Putting values to work: making decisions	74
An ethical base	77

Chapter 3 Time, Stress, Anxiety and Relaxation 79
All you need to know about stress and time management 80
Time management 80
Morning and evening questions 81
Finding the right questions 82
Stress 83
Dealing with life stressors 85
Are you affected by invisible internal stressors? 87
What have you been taught about how to handle stress? 89
Saying 'No' 91
The 'No' questionnaire 92
Anxiety – what is it? 97
Understanding anxiety 98
Do you have the physical symptoms of anxiety? 101
Do you have the emotional and mental symptoms of anxiety? 104
Do you really know how to relax? 108
The relaxation questions 109
Mindfulness 111
How mindful are you? 112
Recognising mindfulness 112
A visualisation exercise 113

Chapter 4 Dealing with the Past 116
Are you living in the past? 118
Your time line 123
Surviving the past 124
What special abilities, insights and skills has your past given you? 125
The transference trap 126
Difficult or uncomfortable memories 129
Difficult memories quiz 130
The myth of moving on 132
Rethink the past 132
Negative life statements 133
Identify and rewrite your negative life statements 135

Being stuck	137
Depression	139
The depression quiz	144
Loss and grief	148
Are you suffering from unresolved or hidden grief?	151
Post-traumatic stress	154

Chapter 5 Happiness, Joy and Creativity — 156

Freedom	157
Curiosity	159
Joy	159
What is your joy rating?	161
Are you unhappy?	162
Building blocks to happiness	163
How happy are you? The happiness questionnaire	165
Keep a happiness journal	171
Exploration and fun	171
Creativity	172
Creative questioning	174
The creativity questionnaire	176
The 'miracle question'	179
Creative problem-solving	181
Well-being	183
Criteria for well-being	184

Chapter 6 Relationships and Communication — 186

Couples exploration questionnaire	188
The relationship phases cycle	202
What phase are you in?	203
Rate your couple communication skills	209
Expectations	213
What are your expectations of a relationship?	216
Positive and negative couple behaviours	216
Rate yourself and your partner	217
Healthy protest	221
Managing conflict	223

Acceptable and unacceptable behaviours	224
Forgiveness and reconciliation	227
Personality differences	228
Are you an extrovert or an introvert?	229
Security and attachment	232
What is your attachment style?	234
The attachment questionnaire	237
Sexual intelligence	242
Explore your sexual intelligence	243
Conclusion: Hope	244
Notes, References and Further Reading	246

'... be patient toward all that is unsolved in your heart and try to love the questions themselves *like locked rooms and like books that are written in a very foreign tongue. Do not now seek the answers, which cannot be given you because you would not be able to live them. And the point is, to live everything.* Live *the questions now. Perhaps you will then gradually, without noticing it, live along some distant day into the answer.'*

– Rainer Maria Rilke, *Letters to a Young Poet*, 1934

introduction

'He who overcomes himself is strong.'

– Tao Te Ching

Knowing helps being. Being self-aware helps us develop ourselves, improve the art of living and feel connection with others. It helps us improve the quality of our lives and those of the people around us. This book will help you develop certain types of self-awareness. By answering the questions you will open up your awareness, make connections, push beyond some of your current limitations, and make new discoveries about who you are and who you can be.

Don't make yourself work through the book from beginning to end, but choose the parts that seem to talk to you now. On the other hand, if there is a section that you really don't want to look at, it might be interesting to explore your resistance. If you have a strong reaction against some of the topics, there might be a good reason. This could be part of the story you have told yourself about who you are and what you can and cannot do – based on the past. This book is interested in bringing you up to date with the here and now of your life. Once upon a time we all had certain limits placed on us, and we learned to work within a belief system that told us what we could or could not do, dare or believe. The fun and challenge of this book is that it gives you ideas and tools to open up your personal Pandora's box of attitudes, behaviours, emotions, thoughts and beliefs. You can choose the ones you want to keep, change or discard. You can challenge yourself, grow, change, develop – all at your own pace. You can gain reassurance, confidence and enhanced self-esteem. There is a wealth of information here for your use, in a straightforward and accessible format.

Overcoming yourself is more than half the battle with any problem. We are very clever at creating problems that then take us decades to figure out. Sometimes other people cause us problems, especially when we are children, and it takes a long time to climb out of the particular trap we find ourselves in. As a psychotherapist I have had privileged access into the inner worlds of many hundreds of people. They have shared their problems, joys and secrets with me, and instead of blaming others, have been especially interested in what it is they might be doing to keep making things go wrong. This book is the result of some persistent questions I have asked myself over years of listening to people who were in some way dissatisfied or unhappy.

How and why do people mess their lives up, and how can we all stop doing it? Why can't we be happy and fulfilled? What is preventing us having what we truly desire? Of course there are all kinds of external reasons why things go wrong and maybe the world is a bad, dangerous and difficult place. At some point, difficult or even impossible things happen to all of us; the only choice you have about this is what kind of attitude to take when something challenging does happen. But the fact that bad stuff happens isn't what this book is about. The book is here to help you make the most of your life whatever happens. It is about developing yourself as a resource that will not fail you however tough things get – and that will enable you to have joy and happiness as well.

A new oracle of change

Many times we turn to various different ways of trying to read the future. The old oracles, such as the *I Ching* or tarot, help us obtain some perspective on difficult and perplexing problems and questions. These ancient oracles are still highly popular. However, they evolved in cultures very different from our own, and represent values, such as the depiction of the fixed roles of women, that may no longer be helpful to us. This book offers a fresh look at *our need to ask questions* and find the right answers for ourselves. While respecting and appreciating traditional wisdom, it also offers a straightforward contemporary approach based on consistent, logical principles. Asking ourselves questions is a powerful way to drive our lives forward.

Why you don't need a fix

It is easy to feel vulnerable and insecure, and to feel that someone else out there must have the answers for you. It is not particularly difficult to train as a counsellor, a life coach, or a seminar leader, and to offer people solutions, models and advice as to how they can tweak their life into shape. Are these people really better experts on you than you are yourself? Sometimes it can be reassuring and comforting to enlist professional help, and there are times when therapy of various kinds can really help you address stuck issues and move ahead. Sometimes another person's feedback is essential to help you see yourself more accurately and clearly. However, it is unhelpful to assume that there is something wrong with you that needs fixing. Many people are trying to sell you something you can't really get from anyone else: a good attitude, and *the ability to ask yourself the right questions*. This is what this book is about.

The 1000 Most Important Questions You Will Ever Ask Yourself takes a different approach to psychology than those you may find in many other popular psychology and self-help books and programmes. It doesn't focus solely on changing your behaviour or challenging outmoded negative beliefs – although this is included. The quiz format is designed to help you bring new awareness to your underlying values, attitudes and emotions. Awareness itself is transformative. You will find the questions continue to work on you long after you have put the book down. Thus, the quizzes have a 'soft' format and do not have routine psychological profile answers. They are designed to help you refresh your mind.

The trap of negativity, complaining, hopelessness, low self-esteem, guilt and self-blame

Sometimes it is amazing that we ever get out of bed at all. Why bother? Overcoming yourself is more than half the battle. It can take tremendous work to create the right attitude in yourself so you are ready for the good things to happen. Often it isn't the problem itself that is the problem, but the attitudes we insist on hanging on to. It will not be possible to read this book without shifting your attitude at least a little! If you are not ready yet, creep back into bed, but remember this persistently cheerful and determined book will be waiting for you.

Why should I?

Why should you bother with all the questions in this book? It seems like a lot of work, and how do you know it will make any difference? Try it and see. Try applying the process to one small area of your life. Try something that seems relatively easy and unthreatening. Then build on your success. Don't start with a huge issue you have been fighting with for decades.

Thinking

An unusual psychiatrist, Wilfred Bion, developed his ideas partly as a result of working with traumatised soldiers after the Second World War. He found that some people will go to extraordinary lengths to avoid thinking about something they don't want to face up to. They block it out and keep it in a separate compartment of their mind. In addition to this, some people unconsciously prevent others from thinking freely or challenging them with thoughts and ideas they don't want to hear.

Bion became fascinated by the actual thinking process itself. What enables us to think our own original thoughts and work things out for ourselves, and what prevents this? Why is it sometimes so difficult to think clearly? Partly it is because we are not taught conceptual thinking tools at school for some reason – perhaps the kids would figure out they had better things to do than stay in school. Partly it is because we are trained to keep blocks to thinking in place so that we don't question reality too much. And partly because we are terrified of actually knowing what we want. It is possible that we all have unconscious or 'unthought' thoughts that are just waiting for us to learn to allow them in. Some of these can be liberating and creative.

Bion developed a concept he called 'Minus K', which is the force within each of us that would like to keep us in the dark. This is the self-saboteur, the resister, the one with all the excuses who wants to stay small and afraid. Bion contrasted this with 'O', the unknowable force for growth and development that also exists within – the unstoppable process of human potential. Carl Rogers, the famous psychotherapist, described this using the analogy of potato shoots growing in a dark basement. No matter how far it was, in time those little shoots would find their way to the light. If we can get enough light and space, we all naturally grow, mature and blossom.

Do I deserve this?

Isn't getting what you want selfish? You don't deserve this, you should think of other people first, you should put your family first, you are not good enough to get the things you want in life. This is an old message of fear, constriction and limitation. Other people might be envious if you have a happy life doing exactly what is right for you. They might not approve. Who do you think you are to have such fancy plans?

If you ever catch yourself having this type of thought, it's time to take yourself in hand. You are not on the planet to fulfil other people's agendas for you. You are here to fulfil yourself, and no one but you can know what that could look and feel like. It could be totally different from what you think being happy and fulfilled 'should' look like – or how it would look to someone else. There's an insistent voice inside you that does know what you want to do and how you want to be as a person. Have you listened recently?

Denial and excuses

You have experienced other people using these, and no doubt you have your favourite versions. You don't have time. You are too busy just making money and surviving to cope with anything else. Your mother wouldn't like it. Rats ate your homework. You have to lose weight before you can be seen dead in the gym. What's your current favourite excuse? You won't be needing it any more. If this is too scary, put the book away for a bit until you can get used to the idea that you won't ever have to pretend to be something that you're not. Once you have been through the questions in this book you won't ever have to defend, justify or explain yourself to someone else.

Denial is something we all engage in. Often it's healthy. We don't want to cope with everything all the time, and sectioning off certain anxiety-provoking thoughts and realities can help us get on with life. On the other hand, denial can become a habit. You must have met people who seem to be able to deny something that is obviously true, because it is just too painful and inconvenient to let this piece of uncomfortable reality spoil the day.

However, some people can go for years and years denying something that is obviously bothering them. Instead of facing up to how bad they feel about it, they hope it will go away. This strategy of ignoring doesn't work in the long term. There is a psychological law – invented by Freud himself – that everything that is denied, ignored or suppressed eventually comes back. The skeletons in the closet do not simply dissolve and become invisible. They gather dust, and eventually someone finds them. We are physically incapable of losing things that have happened to us. They return, perhaps in a form that is not immediately recognisable, such as psychological and emotional difficulties or physical symptoms of stress. This is part of the reason why some therapeutic or self-help approaches may work well in the short term, but in the long term you need something more than positive thinking and behaviour change to transform the way you really feel deep inside.

How this book works

This book offers a toolbox of original, practical and elegant concepts and solutions that you can apply to any situation. You can use it to analyse why things went wrong, but best of all you can use it to refine and clarify your personal lifestyle, goals and dreams – and to solve daily problems. Instead of talking you into having positive, sensible, happy thoughts, the process of asking yourself questions enables you to work things out in a way that is realistic and practical. You don't have to 'think positive thoughts'; instead you are enabled to clear the way to the natural positive thoughts you would have if your levels of stress, your environment and your conditioning did not limit you so much. You will *choose* positive thoughts. You will become more positive, energised and healthy, if you feel ready for this.

In each section, you go through a special thinking process. You will learn to expand problems to more abstract concepts by asking yourself questions. If you can reframe a personal problem or concern into a helpful concept it becomes easier to manage. Because you have a conceptual handle on it you don't have to take it so personally and get so emotionally involved. You can separate the wood from the trees. Once problems and issues have been turned into more abstract values and qualities, they become much easier to work with. They are not so awkward and upsetting. Then, you work backwards step by step to apply your answers to the questions in the situation that concerns you. If this sounds hard, it isn't; but it will take some time and thought and it is a step-by-step process. A good time to work through some of this book might be when you have a chunk of free time, perhaps when you are away from your usual routine.

Don't laboriously work through the book from beginning to end. Choose one section that seems interesting, and work from there. If you only want to do one section, choose Chapter 2, 'Choose Your Values' – this will have an impact on all areas of your life.

Note: A grey strip on the edge of the page indicates a questionnaire or a section requiring your active involvement.

chapter 1
ask yourself

'Life is what happens to you while you're busy making other plans.'

– attributed to John Lennon

What do I really want?

What do I want? This is a dumb question. Of course you know what you want. Or do you? How many people do you know who decided what they wanted and went for it and are now very pleased with themselves? How is it that some people end up with exactly what they want and other people don't quite get round to it? Try asking people this 'simple' question and you will find that an astonishing number of people haven't given it much thought for a long time.

It can be scary to define what you really want – you might get it, or you might have to put yourself on the line and take a risk that it might not work out – or it could work out and you would have to make some changes. It feels like the easiest thing to stay just exactly as you are and not change anything. Except that it's easy in the short term, and very hard in the long term, to feel frustrated that you have not achieved something that you were capable of, that you didn't realise what opportunities you had until they went away again, that you never appreciated what you had until you lost it.

What do I really want? is a scary question, and it would be nicer just to ignore it. It never goes away, however. It is one of those insistent questions – like 'Is there life after death?' – that follows you everywhere you go, like a devoted puppy. It's there in every moment. Not realising that you don't know the answer to this question leads to a great deal of confusion and unhappiness. You say yes to things you don't want, and no to things you do want – simply because you don't realise you must pay attention to this crucial question *every day of your life*.

Try asking the question now. *What do I want?*

Allow yourself space to pay full attention to this question. Give yourself some time to breathe, to centre yourself and see what comes to mind. As answers come, note them and wait and see if anything else arises. Imagine yourself in different situations in your life, for example at work or with your lover or on holiday. In each situation, run through the question again. Let answers come to you from deep down; even if they don't appear to make any sense at the moment, just write them down. Imagine that you have a unique and individual purpose in life, and you are clear what this is. How does this feel? How does it look? How does it feel to be this person who knows what she/he really needs and wants, and who is confident about working towards it?

ASK YOURSELF

> *'The important thing is not to stop questioning.'*
>
> – Albert Einstein

You can use this book to tackle issues and problems, and you can also use it to help you generate new ideas. Asking the right questions gives you a framework for dealing with issues that might otherwise be overwhelming. The human mind simply can't cope with the complexity we are faced with day to day – until it is broken down into bite-sized chunks. Asking the right questions is the difficult part in any problem-solving or creative process. Albert Einstein is said to have been asked what he would do if he had one hour to save the world from nuclear destruction. His answer was that he would spend the first 55 minutes analysing and understanding the problem, and the last five minutes coming up with ideas. He might not have saved the world in time, but he would have come up with some completely fresh, new ideas.

Einstein also said that no problem can be solved by thinking with the same attitude you used to create the problem in the first place. His actual words were, 'Problems cannot be solved by thinking within the framework in which the problems were created.' You have to step up a level in thinking to get an overview, and one of the best ways to do this is through asking questions. Asking the right questions helps you accurately define and analyse the problem. You start to clear away the misconceptions and assumptions that restrict you. You can think in a fresh way that helps shift you out of the rut.

Asking questions is a way of making sure you are focusing on the right problem.

Anthea picks up this book because she is feeling generally a bit low. She thinks this is caused by her two-year-old relationship with her boyfriend, George, who insists on going on frequent skiing trips during the winter months with a group of mates. He leaves her at home because she can't really afford to go, and she is not that keen on skiing. Unfortunately, she gets quite depressed in the winter. (Seasonal Affective Disorder or SAD syndrome affects a lot of people, who feel low moods in the winter due to a lack of mood-busting full-spectrum sunlight.) This reinforces her tendency to feel unwanted and that he has deserted her because he has

23

much more fun without her. She thinks that when he gets back she is going to ask him to make a commitment to marry her, or else she is going to end the relationship. But on getting home with her book, Anthea finds that the 'Relationships' section is quite near the end of the book, and that first she is asked questions about her own self-esteem and level of depression. This puts her into a different frame of mind. She can think about the problem from the point of view that there are things she can do to improve how she feels, rather than wait for George to get back. Reluctantly she has to accept that George's enjoyment of skiing is not the cause of her feelings of insecurity. This feeling – which she usually feels in relationships – has its own roots, and needs to be understood and dealt with before she is ready for a relationship in which two people can have space to explore their independent interests.

How do you know when you are asking the right questions? It's impossible to be sure, but one thing you can do is challenge all your underlying assumptions about a problem, or about something you would like to improve. The skill lies in being able to decide on the exact cause of the problem.

George thinks he wants to be a writer, and in fact he would be a writer if he had time to write. The problem is that he has no time, and everyone keeps making demands on him, including his girlfriend who is very possessive. He feels so stressed out about this that all he can do every afternoon when he gets home from his routine office job is make himself a coffee and feel depressed about how his whole life is a boring uncreative rut.

What he could do is answer all the questions in the 'Time management' section in Chapter 3 to find out where exactly all those precious minutes are vanishing away to. For example, he could find that he spends about five hours a week having those depressed coffee moments. Within two years he could write an entire book in five hours a week if he were organised enough. So now he has to accept that the problem isn't really about time at all. The question is a bit more complex, and he starts wondering if he really wants to be a writer. Actually, what he enjoys most is skiing, and he is not going to give that up, no matter what. In fact, it's his day job that is killing him, and he would love to be an expert ski instructor and perhaps write for people who want to perfect their techniques and get the same incredible sense of achievement he gets skiing off piste. He starts to get excited about a whole new direction he could take. The real problem, he admits, is that he has believed – because his father told him so and he hates to upset his father – that he needs the security of his job, as a consultant on an advice hotline for a software company. He's good at the job and popular with customers, but in truth he is only doing it for the money. His other passion is designing software, which he loves to do in his spare time. New options are beginning to open up, and it starts to become clear that one of the things he has to do is stop trying to please his dad by having a 'steady job'; he is not in fact a 'steady job' kind of person, but he is afraid of challenging his father's view of the world and stepping out on his own. Or is he? Now he has realised this, perhaps it doesn't have to be so difficult. He could find lots of ways to make money, all focused around the things he is really passionate about, as long as he is prepared to travel and make changes.

So George's assumption that he 'doesn't have time' to be a writer is a convenient way of saying he's scared of the real freedom that could come with taking some risks. In fact 'not having the time' in George's case is a kind of resistance to facing the underlying issues. He is resisting discovering his potential.

The right questions for George to be asking himself might be 'What am I most afraid of, and why?' and 'Do I want this to limit me for the rest of my life?'

The life questions

This is the hard bit. You could skip this section, or come back to it when you feel like it. However, this section is really short and won't take long. Have you ever really answered these questions? Has anyone ever asked you these questions? What happened for you when they did?

You can apply these questions to any area of your life you choose.

- Am I happy?
- What would my life look like if one day I woke up and all my deepest dreams were fulfilled?
- What do I do in my life to actively prevent this happening?
- How positive and optimistic am I?
- How do I express my creativity and put it into action?
- What are the special things I have wanted to be or do since I was a small child?
- Do I know what I really want?
- Do I live in accordance with my personal core values?
- Does my lifestyle allow me to fulfil some of the things I really want?
- Do I feel connected to others and to a meaningful whole?
- Do I have a sense of purpose or direction that helps me feel that who I am and what I do are worthwhile? Are there words which can express this?
- Is there enough adventure and risk in my life?
- What is my characteristic approach when faced with a major challenge?
- How have any major setbacks in my life affected my ability to move forward on my own terms?
- Do I give up too easily?
- What am I most afraid of, and why?
- Do I keep reaching a place where I feel I can move ahead, only to find another obstacle in my path? Describe exactly what happens. How does this pattern keep repeating itself? If this repeating pattern was in a film or a song, what would be the title of the song or of the movie?
- What are the things that most frustrate me on a daily basis?
- What are the things that most matter to me on a daily basis?

Spend time with each of these questions. Reflect on them over the course of a day or a week and see what comes to mind. Make sure you write down your responses, so that you can see the progress and change you make over time. See what happens when you live with these questions in the front of your mind. See what happens when you forget them. Try to prevent these questions having an impact on your life – you'll find you won't be able to.

Action

This is the process of putting learning into practice and actually doing something about it. Often this is where we come unstuck, because it is difficult. Often we spend years hiding under the duvet or distracting ourselves with mindless activities rather than experience the pain of a new challenge. Action is a feedback experience. We learn from our experience, then we act on it. Without the action, we don't learn anything new except how to continue surviving in our current state. After you have answered a set of questions in the book, you need to conduct your own scientific experiment. Test out new attitudes and ideas for yourself, and see if they help. If things aren't working out, go back and have another look.

Mistakes

When we take action, we always make mistakes, and it's important to have a good attitude towards mistakes. Mistakes are an integral part of learning: they teach us what we need to learn. As Miles Davies once said, 'Do not fear mistakes; there are none.' If you don't make mistakes, you are not learning anything new. People who think you should know how to do something perfectly almost immediately are making a fundamental error that can prevent learning in both themselves and others. There is no end to the new things you can learn from your mistakes.

What do *you* want to get sorted?

Try your own action research and set some new activities in motion. Then evaluate the effects on your life, and adjust things so that they feel right.

Setting priorities is important when you want to move ahead. It gives a focus so you know what it is you are really meant to be attending to in the midst of all the mundane things that you have to get done and all the demands other people place on you to get their needs met. The important thing is that these are your own real, personal priorities, and not ones that are about fulfilling someone else's idea of who you should be and what you should do.

Action Planner

Your completed Action Planner is your contract with yourself to help you keep on track and achieve your priorities without getting sidelined by other distractions in life.

You need to review it frequently, and make adjustments when your situation changes. Things that you don't manage to complete within one timeframe need to be moved along to the next slot so you don't forget about them.

If you use your Action Planner for one year, you will be impressed by how many things on it will have fallen into place. Once you really decide to do something and make it a priority, it is amazing what you can achieve, step by step. *(Songbird Close)*

Write out your action planner

What are the ten things you most want to change, or take action on in your life, that are your real personal priorities? Some of these may already be in progress, and others may require adjustments, or perhaps something entirely new.

Now

1. Looseing weight & good health.
2. Saving money (PHD)
3. Leaving NZ — so to Europe
4. Having true intechuall writing friends
5. Making a living out of writing
6. Stop teaching EFL
7. Calm, positive mind lots of self belief.

8. publish writing

9. make lots of money

10. Return some of the money into good practical ~~causes~~ areas to help people eg in India]

Over the next two years

1. Leave NZ

2. Publish

3. Start PHD

4. Learn another language

5. Buy our home

6. Have pet

7. Visit Britain

8. Sort sex thing out

9. Have new job

10. Have a deeper philosophical understanding of life

Over the next five years

1. Publish
2. Win awards for writing
3. Sell filmwrights to my books
4. Buy house in Italy
5. Study horticulture — build herbal garden
6. Travel
7. Have a lot of interesting friends
8. Finish PHD
9. Start ("good works")
10. ~~build~~

Long term

1. Pay off mortgage
2. travel around the world
3. be absolutely financially secure

ASK YOURSELF

4 _artistically fulfilled_

5 _happy, serene + healthy._

6 _Connection with God._

7

8

9

10

What specific actions do you need to take to work towards achieving these priorities?
These actions need to be specific, realistic and achievable within the time frame.

Date   **Completed**   **Not yet completed**

Today   _Commit to the belief that change is possible._ ☐ ☐

This week   _Intectual stimulation via film festival_ ☐ ☐

This month   _Two weeks off_
Send work off
Finish Mr Kay ☐ ☐

THE 1000 MOST IMPORTANT QUESTIONS

This year Make the necessary steps to have her an agent, study craft.

Next year Build a more fulfilling intellectual life, save money.

Long term Commitment to artistic excellence

How might you sabotage or delay any of these actions?

1. Becoming depressed, losing hope

2. Overwork

3. Becoming ill

4. Lack of confidence

5. Lack of focus.

ASK YOURSELF

What can you put in place to help you keep on track?
(For example, share your Action Planner with a friend who can help you keep to it, or tell everyone you are going to the gym three times a week, so you feel embarrassed if you don't show up.)

1 life coach

2 buddy meeting / mum

3 daily life-coaching (self) + philosophy.

4 writing mentor

5 Connecting with the life I want outside of NZ.

Confidence and self-esteem

Self-esteem and self-worth

Self-esteem can be defined as believing in yourself and having self-confidence, self-respect and a positive attitude towards yourself. Good self-esteem is fundamental. It is the magic quality that attracts good experiences and the things you want. A negative self-image prevents you getting what you deserve; it also creates havoc in relationships as it is difficult for someone else to love or respect a person who does not love or respect him/herself. When there are two people in a relationship who both have low self-esteem, it can become even more difficult.

Self-esteem is like money; it is difficult to have too much, but other people may dislike you if you appear self-satisfied or conceited. They may try to take you down a peg or two. Some of us have learned to 'stop showing off' and to be self-effacing. We keep some of our good points and our good feelings about ourselves hidden. We wait for someone else to say positive things about us and give us the praise and recognition we so badly need.

The important thing with self-esteem is to develop it in abundance. If you were not given it in childhood, it is hard work to achieve it as an adult, but it is hard work that is a true investment in yourself. No one else can do it for you. There is no substitute for good self-esteem. Fabulous clothes, accessories and holidays can help you feel good, but if the underlying self-worth is not there, these things only provide a temporary boost.

Self-worth is similar to self-esteem. It is the value you place on yourself. This value is not dependent on the things you do or achieve. It is intrinsic to who you are as a unique and special human being. It is what people most miss after you are gone.

Rate your self-esteem

How much are you worth to yourself?
This questionnaire is in two sections, A and B. Rate each question by circling 1 or 2, where 1 = I agree; 2 = I agree strongly. If you disagree completely, write in a zero.

Section A

1. Do you believe you are a fabulous person with many unique qualities? — (1) 2
2. Do you like, love and care for yourself? — (1) 2
3. Do you enjoy spending quality time with yourself? — 1 (2)
4. Do you speak about yourself to others with respect and appreciation? — (1) 2
5. Do you value all the things you have achieved, and don't worry about the things you are not so good at – you can't do everything? — (1) 2
6. Do you appreciate the way you have overcome so many difficulties? — 1 (2)
7. When someone criticises you, do you listen carefully, think about it, take on board anything that sounds useful and disregard the rest? — 1 2 ○
8. Can you be calm, clear and assertive when people are demanding, critical or difficult around you? — (1) 2
9. Are you good at looking after yourself? — 1 2 ○
10. When someone pays you a compliment, do you accept it graciously? — (1) 2

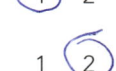

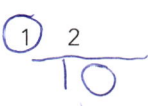

10

Section B

Score this section in the same way, and total the scores for sections A and B separately.

11. Do you feel you have to behave in a certain way with others to make them like you? — (1) 2
12. Do you have to be more generous with your friends than they are with you in order to keep their friendship? (1) 2
13. Do you feel you have to do things you really don't want to do in order to stay in a relationship? — 1 2 ○
14. Do you dress so that you don't get noticed too much or look different? Or, on the other hand, do you invest

a great deal of time and effort in your appearance because you don't feel you would look acceptable without the make-up, clothes, car, etc.? (1) 2
15 Do you find it really hard to say no? (1) 2
16 If someone criticises you do you react either by defending yourself or by taking it personally and feeling hurt and upset? 1 (2)
17 Do you secretly fear that you are worthless, useless, and if people really knew who you were, no one would love you? (1) 2
18 Do you hate being alone in your own company? 1 2 ○
19 Do you frequently and/or consistently engage in activities that you know are self-destructive or harmful to your health and well-being? (1) 2
20 Do you talk about yourself in a negative, complaining or self-deprecating way so that other people don't realise some of your good qualities, or can easily develop a negative impression of you? (1) 2

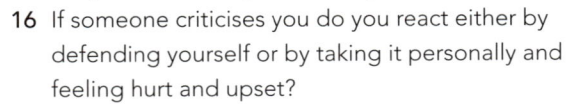

9

Scores
There are two separate sets of scores, for sections A and B.

Section A
15–20
You have outstanding self-esteem and are functioning really well at this level. Either you were parented really well, or you have worked incredibly hard to achieve this. Well done! It is important to remember that very few people have this level of self-esteem, and it could possibly be difficult for you to understand the needs and attitudes of people who simply don't believe in themselves the way you do.

10–15
You have excellent self-esteem. You really believe in yourself, trust yourself, and enjoy who you are as a person. You may have a few insecurities, but this is human. You know how to handle these most of the time. You know that self-esteem is something you have to work at and it is never handed to you on a plate, but you are prepared to make this investment in yourself. You won't tolerate situations for long if they have a negative impact on your self-worth.

5–10
You have worked to develop good self-esteem, and you are well aware of the issues involved in developing long-term confidence and security in yourself. It is possible that some difficult life experiences have adversely affected you, and you may need to put a bit of work into developing more robust confidence so that you can move ahead. You have some good core attitudes towards yourself, and you can build on these by bringing more attention and awareness to the process of increasing your sense of self-worth.

1–5
Although you do have some sound core attitudes towards yourself, you have quite low self-esteem. There must be reasons for this that you are well aware of. It is really bad for your mental health and your general well-being to persist in a state of low self-esteem – it can be part of a self-perpetuating cycle: you feel underconfident so you withdraw, become passive, or hold back, and you don't develop learning opportunities to become more confident. The secret is to practise the behaviours associated with positive self-esteem; if you practise them enough, they start to feel more natural and less like an exercise.

Section B
10–20
You are struggling with low self-worth, and at times you may find life to be really difficult. It is possible you have not developed a strong sense of self-identity, and at times you may have been easily controlled or influenced by others. You are sensitive to criticism or negative judgements. You don't always have enough confidence to take the necessary risks to improve things, and you may be afraid to be alone. Stopping the habit of negative thinking and behaviour towards yourself is a battle.

One thing you can do that will help you immediately is to identify one area where you know you have confidence. Look at the skills, abilities or experience you have developed in a certain area – for example, you know you are good at cooking. Consider how you developed all the skills involved. Try transferring these skills to another area where you feel less confident, but where you would like to succeed. For example, if you are a good cook you are good at learning and storing new information, you have organisational skills, you have creative flair, you are adept at making others feel cared for, and you have the capacity to enjoy and appreciate good things. These skills could all be transferred to a new area you have never tried before; for example, crafts, a team sport or activity, or taking on a new project at work. Gaining new skills is empowering and will automatically help you increase your confidence.

A valuable tip is to start believing it is worth making the effort – even if you don't always know why you are doing it, and even if you don't always feel like it. Confident people act confident, however doubtful they may feel on the inside.

1–10

You have some personal issues connected with low self-worth, perhaps areas of your life or personality that you don't feel entirely comfortable with. These may have been laid down in childhood, and have been reinforced by life experiences along the way. It's never too late to do some repair work and develop a better attitude to yourself. Start with one thing, such as speaking about yourself with pride and respect, or taking better care of yourself and your home environment. Try to get other people to help you. If they don't want to, then you don't need them as much as you think you do. Start to notice the behaviour and communications of others and what it says about their own levels of self-esteem. Then think about how this applies to you. Find people who are relaxed and confident in themselves and learn how they do it.

Seven exercises for developing self-esteem

By spending time on these exercises – although they might initially appear a bit tedious – you will be alerting your mind to something that it really wants you to attend to. You will find you get good results. If some of the exercises bring up some feelings about times when you were made to feel bad, don't worry about this but trust this natural healing process to work itself out.

1. Think about the attitudes and behaviours represented by the questions in Section A of the self-esteem questionnaire. If any of them appear difficult or alien to you, start practising them. If you already do them, practise them some more. For example, try accepting all compliments graciously, and never brush a compliment aside. Try to improve your score in Section A in the next few weeks.

2. Seek out the company of people who are relaxed and confident in themselves. Learn from them and let some of their attitudes rub off on you. At the same time, make sure you spend quality time with yourself each week.

3. As a matter of urgency, avoid the company of people who make you feel bad about yourself, or who like to make themselves feel better by attacking you in some way. You should never permit this. If this is happening to you, it can take some time to gather the strength to do something about it. Practise the other exercises first, until you feel stronger. Don't expect any help from people who prefer you to be underconfident.

4. Write a list of all your good, unique and admirable qualities and abilities. This can include positive things others have said about you. Then act as though you really do believe that they are all true. How would this person act differently to you if she knew that all these things were true?

5. Keep a self-esteem scrapbook or folder. Collect in it all the positive feedback you receive from every possible source; for example, cards and letters with positive messages, references, testimonials or feedback on course assignments. Be sure to write down the positive things people say to you and keep them for your scrapbook so that you can hang on to them rather than forget them. Collect compliments. Make sure you spend time choosing and putting together your scrapbook so that it is something attractive and appealing that you will want to look at and add to frequently. This will become a valuable resource for you whenever you feel down or need a boost.

6. Make sure you develop new skills and achievements on a regular basis so you can always be proud of yourself. Take in and accept compliments, recognition and kudos along the way.

7. Value, celebrate and actively express the ways in which you are unique, individual and different from others, as well as the things that you share.

Self-confidence work-out

Confidence develops through taking risks and putting things into practice. How do you gain in confidence? Are you highly cautious and risk-avoidant, or do you enjoy the excitement and novelty of a certain amount of risk and adventure. If you take few risks, you will become less able to take risks in future.

Remember some good things that have happened to you. These could be anything – a special trip, a long-lasting friendship, a move to a new job or home, having a child, a special achievement, completing an important project. Explore how you personally helped to make these things happen.

List ten good things that have happened to you
These can be from any period in your life.

1. Going to University to study English
2. Travelling
3. Going to NZ
4. My Mew (Chist)
5. Studying herbal medicine
6. ice-skating
7. Yoga
8. Living in Chester Street
9. Writing
10. drama + art + trips around herbal gardens, + historical places

Things you did
Now list all the things you did, and the personal qualities you demonstrated, which contributed to make those particular good things happen. You might have to think hard about this if you think any of these things 'just happened'. What *was* your contribution to helping things to work out?

1. Determination

2. Accepting change

3. Curosity

4. Following dream, our interests

5. hardwork

6. Focus

7. Research + planning

8. Time-management

9. Being open to new experenies

10. ~~help from ot~~ Attaching
    friends to help us
    friendliness

Personal qualities you demonstrated

Personal qualities are things like perseverance and friendliness, or being open-minded, enthusiastic, hard-working or determined.

1. Perseverance
2. friendliness
3. Ability to focus
4. hard-working
5. open-minded
6. Curious
7. high standards
8. ability to plan & research,
9. enthusiasm
10. time-management + courage.

Now take credit for what you did, and how you achieved it. You can achieve more things like this, *and much more* if you hold onto a positive outlook about yourself.

ASK YOURSELF

Plan for success

People do best when they imagine the best outcome, and then plan to make that happen. In order to achieve this, you have to have some clear goals or outcomes in mind. If you don't have the outcome in mind, it is unlikely that you will arrive at it.

What are the outcomes you would most like to work towards? You can also refer back to the life questions earlier in this chapter, and look at the values questions in Chapter 2.

Thirteen successful outcomes

What are the things that would really make you feel satisfied and happy? List some of your hopes and dreams under each section heading. You don't need to spend ages filling this in – this is a quick inventory of your desired outcomes. If you find yourself thinking that something you want isn't achievable, write it in anyway. Just write in a few words under each heading.

This is different from your Action Planner. The Action Planner is about the discipline of setting realistic tasks and achieving them. This is more about the general directions you would like to take. Feel free to be inventive and playful, to daydream.

1. Relationships and family
   meet my sister, supsor child in India

2. Lifestyle
   Healthier, less stressed, less anxious,

3. Travel, leisure, recreation, fun
   Leave NZ, more foreign travel

4. Education, learning, new knowledge or skills
   PHD, 'complete study of craft of writing' then just a few books a year.

5. Money
   increased savings - enough for PHD

6. An individual or shared sense of meaning or purpose
   Inner contentment

43

7   Creativity

A book published & some short stories

8   Sexuality

Start!

9   Happiness

Free of depression, PTSD, anxiety

10   Health and well-being

loose weight, more exercise

11   Commitments

Less

12   Work and career

New job

13   Home and location

own home, new location

You should now have a few words written under each of the thirteen 'outcomes' headings. You need to take these same words and write them in under the headings below. To do this, you need to decide which of these is the most important to you, and which are less important for now. Only you can decide 'importance' – all these things are important to you, but some are more special than others.

Most special outcomes

1   *Improve health (physical & mental)*
2   *loose weight*
3   *leave NZ*
4   *Publish*
5   *Save money*
6   *New job*

Other important outcomes that have to take second place for now, but which I will keep in mind

1. Sponsoring child in India
2. Start PHD
3. Sex
4. ~~Friends~~ own home
5. Less commitments
6. Inner contentment
7. Sister

Congratulations! You have simply and painlessly put your life back on the drawing board and decided what direction *you* want to take in the things that matter most to you.

Now that these outcomes are clearly on the map, whenever possible you are going to make decisions and choices that help you move towards your desired outcomes. At the same time, you are going to step back from the things that push your outcomes further away.

Difficulties may come if some of your outcomes are in conflict; for example, if you want to have babies and make lots of money in the same time period. When this happens, unless you have boundless energy, you will need to re-prioritise your desired outcomes so that you focus on *either* the children *or* the money in the first few years – but you can work on both in the long term.

Self-sabotage

Are there ways in which you limit your own success, get in your own way, and generally screw things up for yourself? Are you a self-saboteur? Do you procrastinate and muddle along?

What does this mean? Either your life has taken some very unexpected turns, in which case your values and goals could have changed quite radically, or you might have tried to slow things down because of self-sabotage factors. These factors do not, of course, include sabotage that happens to you from the outside, which is not your fault.

The self-sabotage factors

How many of these can you honestly say you have never at any time been guilty of?

- negative self-talk, such as 'I can't do it' or 'I'm not good enough'
- low self-esteem
- low confidence
- a sense of unworthiness, or that you don't deserve good things
- low expectations
- confused priorities
- unclear values
- disorganisation
- procrastination
- fear of success
- fear of failure
- fear of making decisions
- blaming others, or blaming circumstances
- making excuses, and believing your own excuses
- avoidance of pressure, competition or any discomfort
- guilt
- fear of making the wrong decisions
- being afraid to ask for what you need and want
- being unwilling to ask for help
- being too isolated and not sharing your thoughts and feelings
- being too patient and tolerant of bad conditions or bad treatment
- fear of what other people might think
- being unable to say 'no'
- being in relationships with others who have their own ideas

about how you should spend your time
- putting your own real needs last
- self-delusions
- denial that there is something that needs fixing
- spending time with people who don't believe in you
- allowing others to take advantage of you
- fear of what other people might think
- feeling victimised, passive or helpless and that there is nothing you can do to improve things

How many of these factors can you admit to?

These factors can be single-handedly responsible for preventing you having the life you need and deserve. Just becoming aware of them can make a huge difference, and this can be the beginning of a whole new attitude. These are the real bad guys in your life, and you can kick them out.

Self-sabotage is often called 'being your own worst enemy'. It results not just from all the negativity, bad feelings and bad experiences in our lives, but from what we tell ourselves about those experiences. We are self-sabotaging when we go round the loop of negative thinking over and over, tell ourselves something isn't really worth the effort, or that fabulous things only happen to other people. Often this is the result of childhood conditioning. We learn to expect little, we feel helpless in the face of life's problems, and we try to soothe and distract ourselves so we don't have to feel sad or bitter or angry about what we haven't got.

The best treatment for self-sabotage is optimism and hope, combined with a willingness to see that it is largely our own depressed attitudes, repetitive negative thinking and unchallenged attitudes from the past that hold us back.

Linda worked as a dental nurse. She was good at her job and the patients really liked her warm personality. The dentists enjoyed working with her. They offered to pay for her to go on a dental hygienist training course so she could run the hygiene surgery. She talked it over with her husband. They both decided it wasn't a good idea. Linda would have to travel to the course each week, and it would mean long hours, studying at weekends, and not always being back in time to cook the evening meal. Perhaps her husband felt a little uneasy that she would eventually be able to earn more than him. He told her she needed to be home for the kids each evening as he was often going to be working late.

In this example, both people in the couple are sabotaging Linda's development and increased financial independence. It is much more comfortable for them to continue at their existing level of income and skill. Years later, they are still doing the same jobs at the same level. They still have to be careful with money, and Linda is beginning to feel the first stages of empty nest syndrome with the kids leaving home. This is something Linda agreed to, to maintain the status quo rather than risk rocking the boat.

How much do you sabotage yourself?

For each of the following questions, choose which one of the four options, **A**, **B**, **C** or **D**, is most like you.

1 You decide you are going to save money to go on a course to upgrade your skills, which will help you earn about half as much again as you do at the moment. The course will involve some hard work in your own time, and there is an exam at the end. What are you most likely to do?

A You put the money aside in a separate account, and make sure you put the time aside well in advance. You complete the course.
B You put the money aside and book out the time, but you find the course really boring so you might miss some of the sessions. You don't do all the homework, so that getting through the final exam becomes stressful.
C You try to fit the course in, but you have got too much else going on, and you decide to complete it next time around.
D Your friends offer you a place on a fabulous trip and you really have to go, and you spend the money you have saved on the trip instead.

2 Your house or flat is a pigsty, your mother is coming, and you just have to clean it up. How are you most likely to handle it?

A You put two evenings and a whole Saturday aside, get in supplies, turn up the music and you blitz the place.
B You leave it to the last minute, but you do a pretty good job, even if your mother arrives while you still have a duster in your hand and all the ironing is piled up on the sofa. When she arrives you are cheerful and make her a cup of coffee and make it clear you have been busy.
C When she arrives, the place doesn't look much better than before you started, because you began cleaning out the kitchen cupboards and finding things you'd forgotten all about. You make some excuses for the mess.

D It's not your problem your mother is a tidiness fanatic. You do a quick vacuum, put the newspapers in a pile, and leave it at that.

3 You would really like a special party for a big O birthday that's coming up. You would love to celebrate in style with friends, many of whom live at least a day's journey away. Which would you be most likely to do?

A Book the venue and send out invites a couple of months ahead so everyone has a chance to book it into their schedules.
B Let everyone know it's happening, book the venue when you know most people can come, and tell people the exact time and place when you talk with them on the phone.
C The party happens, but you didn't invite that many people because you were afraid they might not want to come all that way just for a birthday party.
D You fantasise about the party but it never gets off the ground because it seems like too much hard work to organise. You end up going out for a drink with a few mates.

4 You're doing really well in your job and your manager implies you will be first in line for a promotion when a colleague leaves in a few months' time. Which of the following do you do?

A Work extra hard to prove your worth and how indispensable you are.
B Carry on as normal but make sure you are making the right impression with the right people.
C Carry on as usual – and hope that your sterling qualities will be recognised.
D Relax and celebrate in advance with the lads in the office downstairs.

5 You have a secret desire or ambition. This is something you have always wanted. In replanning your priorities for this year, you realise you haven't done much about it for some time. Which do you do?

ASK YOURSELF

A   Clear time and tackle it head-on like you really mean it.
B   Start to tell people about the project and gradually make it more real.
C   Plan to get going on it, but you are very unsure where to start and you distract yourself with lots of other things that you also need to get done.
D   You talk about it a lot, but there are more important things that need your time right now.

6   **You receive an income tax demand. You had forgotten all about it, and now it's due in a few weeks' time or you will have to pay a fine. Which do you do?**

A   Get it sorted as soon as possible.
B   Worry about how you are going to find the money, and get it together just in time.
C   Put it on the general 'to do' pile on your desk and hope for the best.
D   You don't want to think about such a depressing subject. You would rather pay the fine than feel hassled by it.

7   **One day you notice there's a slow leak from the cistern in your house. Which of the following do you do?**

A   Ring round till you find a plumber who agrees to come straight away.
B   Get your brother or a friend to come and look at it for you.
C   Try to fix it yourself temporarily, but you are not confident about your plumbing skills and you worry about what to do.
D   Put a bucket under it and hope it will go away.

8   **You've got an important deadline coming up. Which scenario sounds like you?**

A   You have been steadily working towards it, and you expect to finish a few days ahead of schedule.
B   You have a last-minute frenzy – you stay up two nights in a row to complete it and then collapse out of exhaustion.

C   You are afraid you won't be able to manage it, and you find yourself worrying about it a lot.
D   You miss the deadline because you don't want to get stressed out about it. You make some creative excuses, and get it done a week or two late.

9   A younger cousin is coming to your town to study, and you tell his family you'll meet with him, take him out for a meal and generally befriend him. However, you are pressed for time with some unexpected extra work and no help at home. Which are you most likely to do?

A   Call him right away and fix an appointment to see him in a fortnight.
B   Call him pretty soon and explain that you are busy but you would love to see him some time.
C   You get around to calling him eventually, by which time you feel guilty; you promise to take him for a day out, and this becomes a source of stress for you.
D   You intend to, but you don't get round to phoning him.

10 When an unexpected opportunity comes along, how do you tend to respond?

A   You make space for it in your life.
B   You do take the opportunity, but it stresses you out as you are already too busy.
C   You get a strange feeling you ought to do something – but you let it slip by.
D   You don't see it as an opportunity.

11 An important project you have been working on is coming to an end. What do you do?

A   Hang on in there; you want to see it through.
B   You complain about the stress, you feel exhausted, but you manage to get it done.
C   You start thinking about your next project, which seems more interesting.

D You're bored and you don't stay around – other people need to finish off the details.

12 You have set yourself some targets for things you must get done over the week ahead. However, some family members or friends make various unexpected and unscheduled demands on your time. They don't seem to realise you are busy and under pressure. Which are you most likely to do?

A Explain you are really busy and that you will get back to them at the end of the week.
B Try to fit in some of their needs as well as your own, and try to get some balance.
C Run round after your family and friends first then attend to your own business if there's time. You feel exhausted and a bit hurt that no one stopped to ask if you were okay.
D Unplug the phone and do nothing.

13 Your boyfriend/girlfriend is jealous and likes to know exactly where you are and what you are doing every day. He/she doesn't like you spending time apart, and always insists on either cancelling your arrangements or coming along when your old mates have agreed to spend an evening together. How would you handle this?

A Make it very clear that your time is your own and you won't tolerate him/her acting as though he/she mistrusts you all the time.
B Try to understand and accommodate his/her point of view, but get increasingly dissatisfied if in spite of your best efforts he/she continues this behaviour.
C You feel resentful but you end up going along with his/her wishes for a quiet life; sometimes you may have to resort to deception to see your old friends.
D You go along with his/her wishes and gradually allow him/her to control who you are allowed to spend time with. You accept that he/she doesn't want you to have a separate social life now that you are a couple.

14 How much do you pay attention to your long-term health?

A You exercise, eat properly, get enough rest, and get any medical or dental problems seen to.
B You take good care of yourself, and generally have a relaxed approach. Sometimes you overindulge, but you keep this within limits.
C You exercise sometimes, eat well when you can, and remember to take care of yourself when you have time. You know you could take better care of yourself, but other things are more important right now.
D You smoke, drink, eat whatever you feel like, don't feel you need to exercise regularly, and seldom pay attention to any physical symptoms even if something is bothering you.

15 How often do you let things pile up, like unanswered or unopened mail, or unpaid bills, so that you end up with a problem that takes much longer to fix?

A Rarely if ever.
B Occasionally.
C Sometimes.
D It happens quite a lot.

Your self-sabotage scores

Number of A's _____ B's _____ C's _____ D's _____

It is possible you may have a mix of A's, B's, C's and D's. If so, you need to read the score results for each item where you scored three or more for any relevant tips.

Mostly A's

You are far more organised than most of the other people around you, and you gain a lot of satisfaction from getting things done. You usually do what you say you are going to do, and you are efficient and reliable. You know you are responsible for yourself and you can't blame other people if you fall short. You have high standards for yourself. You may not always allow enough time to process information or feelings, and so you don't always stop to think about what's driving you. You could afford to relax a little and reassess your values and priorities from time to time, or your goals could be too narrow. You tend to achieve what you set out to do, but you may not always enjoy the journey along the way.

Mostly B's

On the whole you are organised and efficient, and you quietly get a lot of things done. You prefer to have a sense of autonomy and you don't rush around madly in response to external pressures. You take care of things, including yourself usually, and you are also good at collaborating with others. Sometimes it is possible you may feel more anxiety than necessary, for example trying to make things right for everybody else. You can put yourself at the bottom of your list of priorities. You may suffer from stress and exhaustion from taking on too much, and you need to remember to be kind to yourself and to set yourself targets that are realistic and achievable, so that you don't end up with a sense of frustration or failure about yourself. Secretly you may suffer from low confidence, and you need to take a long hard look at the many different ways in which other people appreciate you and your abilities. Don't let yourself be taken for granted!

Mostly C's

You tend to live in a bit of a muddle of unfinished projects and things you haven't quite got around to. In so far as you are a creative thinker, and this is a distinctive feature of your style, this can be an asset as you leave your options open and you can be spontaneous and flexible. However, you would find it really useful to establish your desired outcomes more firmly, and to review this every few months. If you don't, there is a danger you won't complete anything really important to you. There is also a possibility that you have low self-esteem or confidence issues, and that you doubt your ability to succeed. Self-doubt can be a real saboteur for you, and it undermines your potential success. Because of this, you may be limiting your effectiveness in certain areas — that way you don't have to cope with either fear of failure or fear of success. You often underestimate your abilities and feel more anxious than you really need to. You can also feel guilty, and respond to pressure in a confused and confusing way, so other people may not know where they stand with you. You often sideline your own real needs and let the pressure of the moment dictate how you will spend your time. You can easily lose sight of your own needs and well-being. You fit in with other people's needs rather than your own, and may be reluctant to say 'no' to unreasonable demands that you consider to be more important than your own true needs.

Mostly D's
While you have a lot of charm and you always have a creative excuse ready, you are not the most reliable person in the world when it comes to meeting demands and priorities, your own included. You can give a lot of time to the things that are important to you, and are highly skilled at all the many ways in which one can waste time! You resent external demands, especially to do with things that don't really interest you. To protect yourself, you avoid stress and pressure from others when at all possible. You can also engage in denial and procrastination, and because of this you may miss out on a lot of opportunities. It's important that you establish your own desired outcomes and priorities, because you are unlikely to follow through on those imposed by somebody else. Are you still rebelling against someone else's expectations of you? Do you have realistic expectations of yourself, or do you place your goals too high to be achievable, or too low to be worth bothering about? Are you struggling with confused values and priorities? Do you blame others for why your life goes round in circles? What results do you really want? Where do you truly want to be in ten years' time – and how will you achieve this?

chapter 2
choose your values

Chapter 1 focused on setting priorities, goals and action plans, and working with self-confidence and self-esteem. At times it is confusing and difficult to juggle clashing priorities, mixed emotions and the thought that at times you could be sabotaging your own best intentions. This chapter consists of one lengthy set of questions that are fundamental to the success of all the other work that this book may help you set in motion.

What are your values?

Maybe you have thought about this in various ways, maybe you haven't. If you really clarify your values, it means you can be clear about your priorities. You know who you really are and what base you need to stand on to retain a strong sense of yourself. When you are in a difficult situation, you are more likely to know what to do. When life is relatively smooth you can make progress with the things that really matter to you. You get to live your own life, not one that someone else has designed for you.

What is a value?

A value is a guiding belief or attitude that will run your life for you. We all have values, and they underpin and direct our lives. If we don't know what our values are, they run our lives anyway, so you might as well be clear about what they are. You can also make a positive choice to opt for the kinds of values that you like and that make you feel good, rather than the kinds of values we tend to end up with when we haven't taken the time to redefine them.

Often we inherit values, for example from our parents, which are not really relevant or useful to us now. It can be destructive to hang on to outdated values that don't serve us or do us justice. Sometimes our values need to change. Sometimes we need to live closer to our true values – because this is an essential component of a sound sense of self-worth. Different organisations and religions all have their own value systems, which are useful as an organising principle so that everyone knows what is expected of them if they want to belong. In the twenty-first century you have the freedom to choose the security of taking some values for granted, or the creative challenge of questioning old established values, and reinventing your own value system.

Values in everyday life

Jim's parents believed that children, while they should be treated kindly, were not equal in importance to adults, and that children should accept the decisions of adults without question or argument. Jim hadn't really realised how much this had affected him until he had his own children and he heard himself talking to them just as his father had spoken to him. 'Do as I say, and don't argue!' Fortunately, because he is a gentle and kind-hearted man, he listened to his children when they continued to challenge him and insisted he pay attention to their views. Eventually he realised that he sounded 'just like my dad'. He realised he really didn't want to treat his children like this, because he really valued a close, intimate and supportive relationship with them and he didn't want to be a distant and authoritarian father. In fact, he was really upset that they might perceive him in this way. He was just doing it because he vaguely believed that he 'should' treat his children the way his father treated him. Jim is a man who values peaceful, harmonious relationships and has a strong sense of the equality of people, including children. Thus, to act in a way that brought him into conflict with these values would always make him feel stressed. He had to understand how his unexamined, inherited values were in conflict with his own authentic personal values.

Decide on your values

Choose from the lists below, but also feel free to add your own if you have special values that are not included. You are only allowed five top-priority values and five medium-priority values in each category. **You cannot have more than five of each in each section.** This can be difficult. Having to choose only ten values forces you to focus on what really matters to you. The other thing that will happen is that you will find that some of your chosen values are in conflict with others. When this happens, it will be an important clue to areas of your life where you may be experiencing confusion, mixed emotions, or bad results.

When choosing your lists of values, you will find that you will sometimes want to choose values that are in opposition to each other. This is perfectly okay, if you are happy with a busy, rich and complex lifestyle as you juggle a range of different values and priorities. If, on the other hand, you want to downsize and focus on simplicity, you really need to streamline your values so they work together.

If you are in a relationship and you do this exercise as a couple, you may learn a great deal more about each other. It is important that each person in a couple feels free to choose his or her own values even if they are different from their partner's. If your relationship is a place where acceptance and respect of each other's different values is encouraged, the relationship can grow. On the other hand, you need to share certain core values, or you will not have enough common ground. Couples who do well generally accept some influence from each other's values, without allowing them to override their core sense of what is important.

When working on the **family values** section, Barry reflected on the kind of family life he would like to have, but had never had. His parents were quiet, hard-working people who, he felt, never really enjoyed the things they worked so hard to achieve. They valued the family 'being together', but nonetheless family meals were rushed and tense, and everyone had to help clear up as soon as they had finished eating. They rarely spent time hanging out and just enjoying being together. Togetherness meant working hard together. Weekends were spent getting chores done. Even during the holidays they would go and stay with grandparents, which involved spending most of their free time cooking, cleaning and taking the grandparents out on day trips.

For his own family life, Barry chose *happiness, health, sharing, abundance* and *spiritual focus* as his five top-priority values. For his five medium-priority values he chose *connectedness to others, tranquillity, focus on external activity, meaningful education* and *sporting achievements*. He found that some of these values were in conflict with each other; for example, tranquillity and sporting achievements could possibly be incompatible! This meant he had to consider which really mattered the most. He had to make decisions around this to get his life in line with what made him feel good about himself. Putting this into practice involved a time management review.

These values are all equal and neutral. There is not a right and a wrong answer to any of these values questions. But there is what is right for *you*. Over time, you may find that some of your values evolve and change, and it will be worth coming back to this section after six months or a year.

Work your way through these values questions, and you will find that it helps build the effectiveness of the question and answer process throughout this book.

The values list

This is a list of 195 values. In the exercises that follow, you are asked to make choices between these values, to include some in your life and make them a high priority, and to either exclude or de-prioritise others. The lists include many values that you will be in agreement with, some that you will be strongly in agreement with, and some that you will feel neutral about or will disagree with. The important thing is to make your own choices when it comes to values. You shouldn't choose a value because you think it will please someone else, make you a nicer person, or because you feel you 'ought to' be a certain way. Values chosen for these sorts of reasons are not nearly so effective at helping you create the life you want, because when you are under pressure you won't want to stick to them. A value has to be something you feel strongly about or that is personally important to you.

The values are arranged into a number of separate categories, beginning with more abstract and spiritual values and moving on to more pragmatic aspects of lifestyle. As you begin to work through the different sections, you will see that values from some categories overlap with others. This will tend to help you find out and clarify things about yourself. For example, you might discover that several of your chosen values from the different categories include *creativity*, yet you may never have considered you were entitled to make creativity a priority in daily life. If you are not doing anything to actively express an important value in your life, it can be a source of tension, stress, depression and other symptoms.

This exercise will take longer than any of the others in the book – but you only have to do it once, and you will really feel its effects in the following weeks and months. The values listed here may not include some special personal values that are dear to you. There is space for you to write them in. At the end of the exercise you will have your own individualised lists under each of the headings.

To do this you can use the spaces in the book, or keep a separate notebook.

1 Self values

These values are more abstract than practical, and refer to deep, unchanging aspects of ourselves. Look back over many years, and you may find that these are values you have been aspiring to since childhood. Of course you would not have used these words, or even thought about it consciously, but the values themselves refer to timeless qualities that millions of human beings have shared regardless of age or culture.

The 'self values' section is different to the other sections in that you are not asked to select some values and throw others out. You may not want to throw any of these out, or just a few. However, for this exercise and over the next few days, try focusing your attention on just ten of these, and notice what effect this has. Underline or asterisk your ten values, or write them out. What are the fundamental human values that really matter to you?

1 Dignity
2 Self-respect
3 Respect for nature and the environment
4 Respect for others
5 Equality
6 Freedom
7 Love
8 Connectedness to others, or interdependence
9 Autonomy or independence
10 Acceptance and tolerance
11 Compassion
12 Knowing yourself
13 Trusting yourself
14 Living according to your own values
15 Standing up, speaking out or fighting for what is right
16 Playfulness
17 Compassion
18 Peacefulness

19 Serenity
20 Wisdom
21 Others of your own?

2 Spiritual values

There are only ten spiritual values included here. Which ones most help you to feel inspired and uplifted? Again, you don't have to throw any of these out, but focus on the five that are the most productive for you. Add your own, if necessary, to replace one or more of the ten below.

1   I like to have spiritual focus or inspiration in life
2   I practise meditation, or participate in a religion or spiritual tradition
3   Faith is important to me
4   My beliefs are important to me, or a sense that things work out as they should
5   I like to feel connected to a greater whole
6   Life has a purpose, a value, or a sense of direction
7   Life is short – live for the moment
8   It's up to me to make the most of my life
9   I have no particular spiritual focus
10 I have no interest whatsoever in spirituality

3 Personal qualities

What are the personal qualities you like in yourself and that you consider to be your strengths? This section is based on one of the central ideas of positive psychology, which is that you gain better results if you build on your strengths rather than spend time worrying about your weaknesses. Choose the ten qualities which you feel are your hallmark strengths, then choose ten qualities you would like to focus on and develop further. As there are forty items in this list, that means clearing out half the list for now.

1   Patience
2   Tolerance
3   Stamina

4 Confidence
5 Positive attitude
6 Being energetic
7 Being open- or broad-minded
8 Having clear or definite views or opinions
9 Being focused
10 Being divergent, focused on several things at once
11 Having a clear sense of direction
12 Having vision
13 Being dynamic
14 Having personal power, charisma or authority
15 Charm and attractiveness
16 Being flexible or spontaneous and going with the flow
17 Being realistic and sensible
18 Being pragmatic
19 Being stimulating or challenging
20 Being lighthearted or fun
21 Having a sense of humour
22 Being helpful
23 Being supportive
24 Being reliable
25 Being tough minded when necessary
26 Being warm hearted
27 Being a good friend
28 Being efficient and getting things done
29 Being knowledgeable, aware and informed
30 Being capable
31 Being relaxed and easy going
32 Being kind and considerate
33 Being a good family or team member
34 Being hard working
35 Being decisive
36 Being kind
37 Being empathetic or compassionate
38 Being a good listener
39 Being organised or disciplined
40 Being original or innovative

4 Image values

How do you like to be seen? What do you most want other people to admire in you? From this list of twenty-five suggestions, choose how you would most like other people to see, value or appreciate you. Add your own attractive qualities if they have been left off the list, but you can only choose a total of ten values – if you add one, you must remove one.

1. Being popular with everyone
2. Being loved by a few special people
3. Being well loved and cared for and having people to love
4. Being well known
5. Having an instantly recognisable style
6. Being valued or recognised for what you do
7. Being seen as a good, kind, caring, loving or helpful person
8. Being seen as a strong person
9. Being fun or entertaining
10. Fitting in and belonging with those around you
11. Standing out as an individual
12. Being talented
13. Being adventurous
14. Being a high achiever
15. Being a parent of wonderful children
16. Being recognised for the hard times you have been through
17. Being famous or having high status
18. Having a polished social persona
19. What you see is what you get
20. Being an expert or an authority in your field
21. Being someone who can make a difference
22. Attracting attention for the way you look
23. Being admired for your achievements
24. Being a fabulous host or hostess, or being admired for your home
25. Having a special lifestyle

5 Your most highly valued resources

Much of life requires you to make an effort and put energy out. If you are not careful this can get out of balance and you can find yourself running on an empty tank. What gives you energy? What are your most important sources of inspiration, encouragement and nourishment? What enables you to really feel good? Choose fifteen from this list of twenty-five. This is then your list of energising resources which need top priority in any review of your lifestyle.

1. Spending time in nature
2. Solitude, or time alone
3. Listening to music
4. Watching films
5. Looking at art
6. Going to art performances
7. Reading
8. Spending time with a close partner
9. Spending time with children or young people
10. Spending time with relatives
11. Spending time with a mentor, inspiring friend, therapist, teacher or group
12. Studying and gaining knowledge
13. Learning new skills
14. Creative self-expression – list creative activities that you have found helpful
15. Getting good feedback and appreciation from others
16. Spending time on creative activities, such as homemaking or gardening
17. Fulfilling sex
18. Socialising with your friends
19. Working to improve your physical fitness or health
20. Spending time with animals
21. Challenging sports or activities
22. Being pampered
23. Going on holiday or travelling away from home
24. Having a wide network of friends, colleagues and contacts
25. Enjoying a sense of achievement

6 Lifestyle values

These values refer to the question 'What is the best way to run my everyday life?' Again, this is a rare opportunity to stop and consider how you would really like to do things. It's easy to wake up one day and find that you are just going along with what seems expected of you – but did you really choose your current lifestyle? Is it the best one for you, or are you agreeing to put up with it for a period of time to fulfil some important and valued commitments? Or is it something that just happened: one set of circumstances led to another. This section will bring up some areas that may be unresolved; for example, if you don't earn enough money to have the lifestyle you would ideally choose, then you may have decided to settle for a job that is not too demanding so you have energy for other things. Choose fifteen lifestyle preferences from this list of forty. Sorry, but you just don't have time for more.

1 Having a quiet life
2 Having a busy life
3 Having a simple life
4 Working to have good things
5 Making sure you and your family are comfortable
6 Working to achieve wealth and security
7 Working to achieve status or prestige
8 Raising children in the way you believe is best
9 Being child-centred
10 Putting home and family first
11 Finding a balance between home and work
12 Putting work first
13 Putting others' needs first
14 Putting your own needs first
15 Making a contribution to society
16 Working for causes you believe in
17 Work, then play
18 Play, then work
19 Getting things done
20 Being organised
21 Enjoying the process
22 Enjoying hanging out
23 Being spontaneous

24 Developing yourself
25 Nurturing others
26 Having a beautiful home
27 Having beautiful possessions
28 Spending money on travel
29 Spending money on going out
30 Having lots of friends
31 Having a few close friends
32 Having a committed relationship with one partner
33 Being single or having more casual relationships
34 Lots of sex
35 Not too much time and energy spent on sex
36 Saving money
37 Spending money
38 Investing in interests and hobbies
39 Investing in education and training
40 Making changes to your lifestyle

7 Power values

Your power values are the things that help you feel the most effective, free, strong and empowered. Choose five from this list of fifteen.

1   Self-discipline
2   Gaining achievements
3   Being in charge of others
4   Having important responsibilities
5   Being free of responsibilities
6   Being healthy and fit
7   Being effective, or competent
8   Being talented or highly skilled
9   Looking good
10 Having money
11 Having an effective support network
12 Having freedom to make your own decisions
13 Feeling closely connected to your partner
14 Overcoming personal limitations and hang-ups
15 Believing in yourself no matter what

8 Attitude values

These attitudinal values are about your preferences in your basic approach to everyday life. These things are much harder to change, as they are more intrinsic to your personality and your psychological make-up. Choose ten from this list of twenty.

1. Being confident
2. Being positive and optimistic
3. Being realistic
4. Having a good sense of humour
5. Being tolerant
6. Being open-minded
7. Knowing exactly where you stand on important issues
8. Needing plenty of information before you make a decision or complete a project
9. Being accepting
10. Being adventurous or curious
11. Being friendly
12. Being cautious
13. Enjoying taking risks
14. Preferring lots of contact and stimulation
15. Preferring to focus on one thing at a time
16. Saying yes to lots of new experiences
17. Saying no to lots of new experiences
18. Preferring security
19. Preferring change
20. Meeting life full-on

The values work-out

You now have your unique combination of values in a series of eight lists.

If you have been through this complete list-making exercise, you will find a thinking process has been set in motion and this may take time to complete. There is no need to move on to the following exercise until you feel ready. When you are ready, the values work-out is where you apply your values to specific areas of your life.

Use the spaces or your notebook to write ten values under each of these headings. You will need to refer back constantly to the eight values lists you have made. You will see you can choose only fifty values in total. This will force you to choose the ones that really are a priority for you, and to focus your energy and attention on them. This can involve some difficult choices!

1 My fundamental personal values

These values are essential to me, and are non-negotiable.

1. _____
2. _____
3. _____
4. _____
5. _____
6. _____
7. _____
8. _____
9. _____
10. _____

2 I need my lifestyle to reflect these values

1. _____
2. _____
3. _____
4. _____
5. _____
6. _____
7. _____
8. _____
9. _____
10. _____

3 I would like my everyday attitude to reflect these values

1. _____
2. _____

3 _____
4 _____
5 _____
6 _____
7 _____
8 _____
9 _____
10 _____

4   In my relationship with myself and others I would like to think of myself as holding these values

1 _____
2 _____
3 _____
4 _____
5 _____
6 _____
7 _____
8 _____
9 _____
10 _____

5   Values that represent me

I would like significant people in my life to see me as representing these values.

1 _____
2 _____
3 _____
4 _____
5 _____

6 _____
7 _____
8 _____
9 _____
10 _____

6 Values for personal development and success

I would like to place more emphasis on these values to help me achieve my personal priorities and feel good.

1 _____
2 _____
3 _____
4 _____
5 _____
6 _____
7 _____
8 _____
9 _____
10 _____

7 Inspirational values

These are the values that motivate and inspire me the most, and that I would like to refer back to as an everyday guide

1 _____
2 _____
3 _____
4 _____
5 _____

Applying your values

Once you have prioritised your values, the next stage is to think about how to apply them more directly to real life.

Think about **ten practical changes** you can make within the next three months to help put your values even more firmly into place in your daily life. Remember to make these changes effective but realistic. You may also need to think about how you want to handle any conflicts of interest that will arise. This is the essence of the values work-out: what really matters to you?

1 _____

2 _____

3 _____

4 _____

5 _____

6 _____

7 _____

8 _____

9 _____

10 _____

Putting values to work: making decisions

Can't make a decision? Decisions are a test of *values, priorities, strength of purpose, clarity* and *judgement*. Making a decision can be difficult because it forces you to clarify your true values and objectives and commit yourself to a point of view. It is enabling to use any decision-making process, even a small one, to help reinforce your chosen values. Your values are your values, and cannot be reduced, challenged or taken away from you. If you know what they are and live by them you will reduce conflict, confusion and procrastination, and reach your goals faster. Having said this, there are some tough decisions to make, and in some situations it is really hard to make up your mind. There are several different kinds of decision makers. You might be someone who likes to make decisions quickly and get on with it, or you may like to mull over things for a long time. Both these styles have their strengths, but each can let you down.

Think back to a time when you made a poor decision

A poor decision is one that, in hindsight, produced results you didn't like.

Did you decide too quickly or take too long?

___

Did you consider the impact on other people too much or too little?

___

Did you realise the long-term consequences? The short-term consequences?

___

___

How do you think the important people in your life experienced you while you were in the process of making the decision?

___

___

___

What motivations pushed you into making this decision?

Why would you not make this decision again?

What values do you think were driving this choice at the time you made it?

With hindsight, how would you do it differently?

What can you learn from the experience?

Think back to a time when you made the right decision
A right decision is one that brought you results you are still pleased about.

Did you make the decision quickly or take time over it?

What values motivated this decision?

What did the people around you think of your choice?

How did you know it was the right decision at the time?

With hindsight, what were the factors that made this a good decision?

An ethical base

It is extremely stressful to run your life without a considered ethical base. Everything you do has an effect – not just on others, but also on yourself. Each action you take goes towards building the person you will become. At the time, you don't realise all your actions have consequences on the future person you are going to be. When you are younger you think the future can take care of itself. Living within an ethical framework frees you up from having to feel guilty or worry about the consequences of some of your actions. It can make decisions easier, too, as you know the right thing to do in some situations. Without your own code of ethics, you can find yourself adrift on the sea of your own passing moods and impulses, and have no means of setting a chart for your behaviour.

The Buddhist concept of karma, the law of cause and effect, is useful here. In this theory, every action has a consequence. If you accept the idea that there is no action you can take without consequences, it helps you think about the kind of results you actually want. If you want to be thin, every time you buy a bar of chocolate, you will make your desired state of thinness a little less likely.

Building on this philosophy of cause and effect, some Buddhists believe that you yourself will experience what you have done to others – that the experience will come back to you, because we are all part of the same interconnected system. This idea then leads on to a belief that you had better treat people in the way that you would like them to treat you.

Think about something you did in the past year that you are not entirely happy about.

Think about the effect on the other person or people involved.

What about the ongoing effect on yourself? How is this still affecting you?

Think about some positive action you took that made you feel good.

What was the effect on you and the other person or people involved? How is this still affecting you?

Ethical principles

These general ethical principles are guiding values that you can use to think through tricky situations in which there might be a conflict of interests, or where there is a strong potential for people to get hurt. When a problem comes up, try thinking it through using these principles. This type of problem solving comes down to making a series of choices from the list. Ethical principles are not universally applied – for example, resources are generally distributed unfairly, or people may be ethical towards some people and not others.

To start with, consider the first three ethical values:
- Doing good – what will create the greatest good? This could be the most good to the greatest number of people or to one person.
- Respect for autonomy – what gives everyone involved the best opportunity to make their own choices?
- Co-operation with and helping others.

Then make choices from the values in the following table. These can be intensely personal, or applied as a general guideline.

Respect	versus disrespect
Avoidance of harm, or causing the least hurt or damage	versus an action that causes harm or hurt
Speaking positively	versus talk that will have negative consequences, or talk that is thoughtless, such as gossip
Fidelity, or loyalty, and keeping to agreements	versus feeling there are good reasons that justify breaking an agreement or contract
Justice	versus injustice or lack of justice
Fairness	versus unfairness or lack of generosity
Equality and acceptance of diversity	versus treating some people as better or worse than others
Truthfulness	versus deliberate distortion or avoidance of the truth
Taking positive action when required	versus bystanding, not interfering, or sitting back and observing when something needs to be done

chapter 3
time, stress, anxiety and relaxation

All you need to know about stress and time management

Even the words *stress* and *time management* are anxiety-provoking. They seem designed to make you feel inadequate, and that everyone except you has got it all sorted. In one sense, everything practical and useful about these subjects can be written on the back of an envelope, and it is all included here in an accessible form. Although time management, stress and anxiety are completely different topics, they have a direct link with each other.

Most of us run into both stress and time management problems from time to time, as a result of juggling conflicting priorities and the universal unease of 'too much to do, too little time'. We feel we are time-poor. It is inevitable that we will feel stressed, as life is intrinsically stressful, and *this is not your fault*. There are times when things start to slip out of control, and then time management tips can be useful. It is even more useful, however, to make friends with time management and stress busting when things are not too difficult, so that you have something to rely on when life speeds up unexpectedly – which it will. Time is a resource, and we can use it in the ways that suit us best, rather than fitting into and feeling driven by an imposed schedule.

Time management

Most time management techniques are similar: they ask you to establish your priorities and then list things to do in order of their importance, ticking them off as you complete them. You need either a personal organiser, a notebook or a computer program. It is important to write everything down, so that nothing is forgotten. The problem with this kind of system is that it tends to make you feel inadequate if you 'fail' to tick things off on your daily, weekly or monthly planner. And the reason we don't tick everything off on our 'to do' lists every day is that we are busy doing other things that may be equally important, which we haven't written down. The traditional time management technique doesn't allow for the fact that we have to deal with constant interruptions, and a continuous flow of communications and information coming our way, plus the fact that we are often balancing the needs of several other people alongside our own. In addition, this approach can rely on 'oughts', 'shoulds' and guilt – a purely logical approach that doesn't work for a lot of people because it's not a fun or creative way of dealing with life.

The idea that you shouldn't put off till tomorrow what you can do today is a recipe for acting like the White Rabbit in *Alice in Wonderland*, who was always in a terrible hurry and running round in circles trying to go faster and faster. You can't get most of it done today, and lots of really important things will have to be put off until next week or next year. It takes time to work towards your desired outcomes. If you treat time as an enemy that must be defeated, it is not always kind to you – there will always be something else you haven't done, achieved or managed. Why not make friends with time? Suppose there is exactly the time you need to do the things that really matter? Many spiritual philosophies stress the importance of being here now. Simply being present in the moment, and doing what has to be done right now, is enough.

Sometimes it helps to do nothing at all until you have really established your true, heartfelt values, priorities and desired outcomes, because if these are confused, you won't be able to keep to them efficiently, and will waste time with delaying tactics. You won't spend time doing what you think you should, but what you want to do. The result is that you can feel like a disorganised failure. Try spending a day each week or month at home, and don't expect to get much done. Give yourself time to breathe, think and let things settle into place. Use the time to reflect on your goals, dreams, values and your real priorities. Instead of wasting time doing nothing, you will find that this time, where you give yourself permission just to be, breathes new life into the rest of your week.

Morning and evening questions

Get into the habit of asking yourself the right question every morning. This is a bit like Microsoft's 'Where do you want to go today?' It could be:

- What do I really want to focus on today?
- How do I want to feel by the end of the day?
- What are the things I really want to get done today? or
- How can I best help myself feel okay today?

Finding the right questions

Only you can know what is the right question for you. It might change every day, or remain the same for months. Focus on your question while breathing deeply and calmly, and notice how it makes you feel inside. If it makes you feel stressed and anxious, this is a sign that it isn't the right question. The question has to be something about you, about helping you get through the day in the best way possible, and it should make you feel calm. Focusing on the right question will make you feel relaxed, alert and that you are taking control of an aspect of your life.

Just before you go to sleep at night, it's really useful to focus on a question, perhaps something that has been playing on your mind that you would like to resolve. For example, how am I going to tell my mother that we won't be there for Christmas? This gives your subconscious a chance to work on the question as you sleep.

When you wake up, try exploring the question in your journal for a few minutes. Try this for a few days until the problem becomes clearer. Often it is possible to 'write stress off' by writing it out and really exploring, describing and clarifying the problems on paper.

Write down a few morning and evening questions, so your mind can start sifting them while you are busy doing other things.

Morning questions

1 _____
2 _____
3 _____
4 _____
5 _____

Evening questions

1 _____
2 _____
3 _____
4 _____
5 _____

Stress

Why get stressed?
There are all kinds of reasons, which may be unique to you and your situation, but there are some causes of stress that are now clearly understood. People who experience stressful life events tend to become more anxious. A stressful life event includes anything that significantly alters your life, and these things don't all have to be negative – in fact, achieving outstanding success can be an enormous source of stress. Stressful events include marriage, separation and divorce, having a baby, new responsibilities, health problems or loss. Life stressors increase your overall level of stress, particularly if several of them happen within a few years. At the time you may feel you cope okay – in fact, other people may think you have coped extremely well – but there is a price you pay for this. Your underlying level of anxiety can gradually increase. Often this anxiety finally surfaces just when you have managed to cope with all the problems and you feel you should be able to get on with your life.

How stressed are you?
Tick how many of these life stressors have happened *within the past five years*.

1. Death of someone close ☐
2. Being a victim of crime ☐
3. Accident or trauma ☐
4. Divorce ☐
5. Separation ☐
6. Moving house ☐
8. Moving location ☐
9. Any significant loss or change that you did not feel able to control, e.g. being made redundant ☐
10. Significant health problems – either yourself or someone close to you ☐
11. Concern about family members, such as teenagers ☐
12. Legal battles ☐
13. Problems with relatives ☐
14. Serious disagreements with family members ☐

15 Being harassed or bullied ☐
16 Serious financial worries or big changes in financial circumstances ☐
17 Serious worries about your home ☐
18 Problems in your relationship ☐
19 Problems with alcohol or drugs – either yourself or someone close to you ☐
20 Loss of independence ☐
21 Loss of mobility ☐
22 Loss of things you took for granted ☐
23 A significant personal achievement (yes, this can be a cause of serious stress) ☐
24 Much too much to do, more than you can physically cope with ☐
25 Not enough to do, having no sense of purpose, or being bored ☐
26 Problems at work ☐
27 Feeling isolated or lonely ☐
28 Not having time to exercise or relax ☐
29 Children leaving home ☐
30 Falling in love ☐
31 New family member ☐
32 Problems caused by bad weather or natural disasters ☐
33 Persistent difficulty in getting enough sleep ☐

Number of life stressors you have lived through: _____

Even if you only ticked two or three of the above, you have every right to feel life has been tough. However, do you have a right to feel stressed? Stress is not actually caused by these events – even the most incredibly difficult ones – but by our reaction to the situation and what we tell ourselves about it. It's how we handle ourselves in situations that leads to long-term stress-induced problems. It's not the problem itself, but what we tell ourselves about the problem, that counts. That's why some people get incredibly stressed out if they have to take the cat to the vet, and others can manage a company, raise three kids and still find time for a manicure and cooking dinner for eight.

However, if you have experienced *five or more* of the 33 stressors above within the past five years, you are at risk of all kinds of stress-related problems, including low self-esteem, depression, relationship breakdown or stress-related illness. People who try to cope alone without help can end up losing direction, feeling unable to work, or drinking too much. You are vulnerable and need support and plenty of time for relaxation and recuperation – time just for you without feeling guilty about it.

Dealing with life stressors

Many people deal with these life stressors intelligently, but this takes some presence of mind. You may need to change your life radically to take account of your real underlying needs. For example, you cannot afford any additional stress such as an exhausting job or to support others who don't support you back. Even a tiny additional stress can act as 'the straw that broke the camel's back' and make you act like a stressed person: tense, irritable, weepy, over-reacting and touchy, aggressive, exhausted or living with a permanent headache and other psychosomatic symptoms.

Many people are not brought up to be emotionally competent. They can handle big stuff in life, but they have not learned to handle their own emotions. When they feel vulnerable, scared or out of their depth, often the only thing they know how to do is cover up their feelings.

Charlie is a good example of someone who found himself stressed out in ways he was totally unprepared for. He only sought help when things got so bad he realised he couldn't continue. Charlie was a promising rugby player when he was at school and college, and trained hard. Rugby was his passion. He was also a really popular guy and had a great social life. He trained hard and played hard, he was part of the in-crowd, and was visibly rebellious – he would be the guy smoking and drinking well into the night, and it never seemed to affect his performance.

Charlie's life was totally changed by circumstances over which he had no control – things he didn't have a clue how to handle. His father died when he was 19. He coped with this by shutting himself away and not talking to anyone about it – he didn't want to let anyone see his feelings. He felt humiliated by how lost and insecure he felt without his father, and he covered this up. He somehow believed that admitting any 'weakness' would make him look like a failure. His performance started to suffer, because he started drinking even more heavily, and taking any drugs that were on offer.

He realised he desperately needed to sort himself out, and decided getting away from it all for a few weeks could be the answer. His family gave him money for a special trip overseas, and he went on an adventure holiday to South America with three other guys from college. They were mugged at gunpoint, and everything they had was taken off them. Charlie felt humiliated and violated, as if he had been raped. He felt he should have tackled the gunman – instead, he froze. The holiday that was supposed to sort him out turned into a further source of deep distress he could not resolve.

Charlie decided to drop out of college – he didn't feel like facing his peers and friends after what had happened to him. He didn't want sympathy, and he somehow felt that what had happened to him was his own fault, that he should have been able to protect himself. He went back home to live with his mother, who was understanding, but he didn't want her advice and they ended up having rows. He got a mind-numbing job in a factory and spent the evenings and weekends drinking. He hated the fact that he had lost his promising sports career, and this made him drink all the harder to blot out his disappointment in himself.

The saving grace in Charlie's life was a patient and kind-hearted girlfriend who somehow managed to stay with him – although they lived apart – and who eventually managed to persuade him to get help. She said he either had to get help or she would leave him, and he agreed to give it a try as a last resort. His doctor referred him on to a stress management programme. At first Charlie thought it was a waste of time; in the first sessions he was grumpy and uncommunicative, and insisted he felt 'fine'. But in the end he had to admit that some of the course made sense. The best thing was that there were other guys on the course that he could relate to, who seemed relaxed about talking about the bad stuff that had happened to them. He realised lots of other guys had difficult lives, not just him. He saw it was okay to be a man who felt bad about himself, and no one judged him for this. Although life didn't sort out for Charlie for a long time, this was the beginning of his learning a new attitude towards himself. For him this began with accepting the reality that he felt vulnerable and alone. His ideas about how a man should be – tough, distant and unemotional – were spoiling his life just as much as the traumas that had happened to him.

Are you affected by invisible internal stressors?

For Charlie, the loss of his father at a young age when he still depended on him emotionally will remain an invisible source of stress throughout his life. This will colour his perceptions of all the things that happen to him.

There are some things that happen to you when you are younger that have a significant effect on your life ever after. There are some things that never go away. They create additional stress for you when you are in a situation or relationship that for some reason evokes aspects of that early experience.

Experiencing these invisible internal stressors adds considerable extra weight to any stress that you feel as a result of life stressors.

Have you experienced any of these?

1. Parental conflict ☐
2. Parental separation and family break-up ☐
3. Periods of separation from your parents that you yourself did not choose ☐
4. Persistent parental absence or neglect ☐
5. Abuse or bullying ☐
6. Bereavement, especially loss of a parent ☐
7. A traumatic event ☐
8. Lengthy periods of illness or being in hospital ☐
9. Problems at school or college ☐
10. Becoming a parent before you were ready ☐
11. Being singled out as different in some way from your peers (for example, race, sexuality, school ability or disability) ☐
12. Being isolated or lonely as a child or teenager ☐
13. Having to take care of a relative while you were still a child or teenager ☐

14 Having to take too much responsibility for younger siblings, or having a sibling who required a great deal of extra attention ☐

15 Having to relocate at a bad time, or frequent moves of home or school ☐

16 Having to leave home before you were ready, or having to stay at home when you were ready to leave ☐

Score

Number of stressors out of 16: _____

If *more than one* of these happened to you, how is this still affecting you? Have you learned from the experience; for example, if you were lonely as a teenager, has this given you extra insight into the importance of friends and peer group for your own kids? You must have learned a lot from this experience, and you and others can gain from this.

If *two or three* of these happened to you, it is likely that you have overcome much of the unhappiness but it may still affect you if it was severe. For example, if you were neglected by a parent and had no one to protect you, this will always affect you to some degree. Do you know how it affects you now? Have you talked it through with people who love and understand you now? There is a lot you can contribute in terms of understanding the issues involved. If you haven't spent much time reflecting on these issues from the point of view of the age you are now, this would be time well spent in terms of bringing your coping style more up to date.

If *more than three* of these happened to you, you have been served a plateful of long-term stress-inducing experiences. You may have processed and dealt with them well, or you may have forgotten all about them. But whenever certain situations occur in your life which, in some indirect way, remind you of these earlier experiences, the old feelings you had when you were a young person can be restimulated. This can give your behaviour a complexity that other people may not always understand.

Hayley was bullied at school when she was 14 and 15, and when she told her parents they said it's a tough world out there and you have to fight your own battles and stand on your own two feet. Hayley learned it was no use running home to Mum and Dad in the hope that they would support her or sympathise. She found that teachers rarely supported or bothered to help her, either. She learned to distrust authority figures, who set rules but didn't really care about what happened to you.

Now when Hayley finds herself in situations where she needs to be assertive to get the things she needs, she can get quite panicky. She reverts to 'I have to do this all on my own and no one's going to help me' mode. It's as if she believes somewhere inside that she's still on her own, and that she has still only got the resources of a fourteen-year-old with which to take on the world. She has to be reminded that now there are people in her life who are more than happy to help her out.

What have you been taught about how to handle stress?

We have all been given messages about how to deal with stress from those around us. Messages from parents, for example, can be unconsciously absorbed so we don't even realise what attitudes and responses we automatically pull out in response to situations that trigger a stress reaction. Some people also have built-in personality factors that make them more prone to stressing out, while other people just seem to be naturally more pragmatic and laid back.

When we are most under stress, we regress to deeply laid down childish or unconscious habits of mind that relate to our own fears about survival. So when you are stressed out, you are likely to be less rational. You can be irritable, moody or withdrawn. People tell you that you are not being 'yourself', and you know this is true but you can't seem to do anything about it.

What hidden survival messages have you internalised about how to handle stress? Are any of these familiar, or do you have a special version of your own?

Independent stress style
- I have to cope on my own
- Being strong means not showing feelings
- I'm here to make it okay for everyone else
- I can't rely on men/women when the chips are down
- Other people are not here to help me
- Leave me alone
- I can do things much better myself
- I don't want to talk about it, I can handle it

Dependent stress style
- I can't do anything on my own
- Panic – and attract someone else's attention
- I can't cope
- My feelings are out of control
- Act helpless and someone will have to help me out
- Don't abandon me
- I have to control and manipulate or else people won't give me what I need

When you act as if any of these statements are true, you are responding to a hidden blueprint that was laid down in your past, and you won't be thinking clearly.

You can replace these outdated beliefs with something more realistic and useful, such as:
- I can cope when I have the support and help I need
- I can rely on others to help me out when I need it
- I can ask for help appropriately
- I am not alone
- I can trust other people to be there for me

– or write your own!

Saying 'No'

Being able to say no, and mean it, is an incredibly important life skill. Without it other people's needs and whims can take over your life. Stay in charge of your time and avoid stress by saying 'No'. Saying no with confidence, and meaning it, is a great way to stay on track with your own plans and agendas. However, it can be stressful to say no because it means dealing with conflicting desires, commitments and priorities. Are you a doormat, does saying no make you feel anxious, or can you say no and mean it? How successful are you with 'No'?

Your skill with the 'no' word is a good indicator, not just of interpersonal skills, but also of your ability to take appropriate care of yourself and your own needs. There is evidence to support the idea that the people who live longest and happiest are those who don't care too much about what other people think about them, and they don't let other people control and manipulate them more than absolutely necessary. Within reason, they live life on their own terms – which means occasionally saying 'No' in a constructive and friendly way. Being good with 'No' also means you can say 'Yes' when you really mean it. Thinking more about 'No' will also lead to your thinking more about 'Yes'.

So what does your ability with 'No' say about you, and what can you learn from your 'No' style?

The 'No' questionnaire

Choose which answer is most like you – **A**, **B**, **C** or **D** – then add up your score at the end.

1. You have planned to spend the evening getting things done at home – there are some things you have been putting off, and you have finally put aside some time to sort them out. A close friend calls to say she needs you to come over tonight because she is having a relationship crisis and she must talk to someone immediately. Do you:

A   Rush over immediately.
B   Spend time worrying, but decide that her problems are more urgent than yours, and go over after a short delay.
C   Tell her that you will come over but you need to spend a couple of hours getting things done first, and ask if she can make dinner for you both.
D   Tell her that you are too busy today, but you could talk to her some other time.

2. A tele-sales company calls you at home in the evening to sell you a product you do not need. The young woman on the end of the phone is sweet and you don't want to hurt her feelings. Do you:

A   Go along with her sales pitch for about twenty minutes.
B   Go along with it for a few minutes and then say, sorry, you really must go because the dog is being sick.
C   After a few moments, say that you don't have time for this, and no, you don't want her to call back, thank you.
D   Snap at her and put the phone down.

3. You are in a hurry at lunchtime, because there are a few things you really must do, such as take a late package to the post office. A friend calls to invite you to lunch to share some exciting news. Do you:

A   Meet her for lunch, and hope that somehow you will fit it all in.

TIME, STRESS, ANXIETY AND RELAXATION

B   Meet her for lunch but keep looking at your watch and stressing out.
C   Agree to meet her but say you're sorry you only have half an hour.
D   Say you are too busy today, but could you make another date.

4   Your sister or best friend asks you to babysit at short notice so she can go out with a new lover. Do you:

A   Agree right away, like you always do.
B   Feel a bit used but agree anyway.
C   Say you will do it this time, but that you can't always be available.
D   Say you have a busy life too, and you can't do it today.

5   A guy at the office has been saying for some time that you must have lunch together to discuss things you have in common. You are alone in the office together and he puts pressure on you to agree to do it one day this week. Do you:

A   Agree to go without giving it a moment's thought.
B   Have some misgivings, but agree to go as you don't want to hurt his feelings.
C   Go along, but try to keep the conversation on work topics.
D   Make it clear you want to keep a professional distance and will not meet with him socially on his own.

6   You get to the restaurant where you have booked a lunch date. You only have an hour. When you arrive, a waiter tells you there has been an overbooking and there will be a short wait for a table. The place looks busy. Do you:

A   Sit down and wait, and hope your table won't be long.
B   Ask exactly how long you will have to wait and explain that you are on a schedule.
C   Say you don't have time to stay, and leave.
D   Complain about the mistake and then leave.

7   You have signed up for an evening class that you are really looking forward to. Then you find that your partner expects to be able to use the car on that evening, and that he thinks his need is more important than yours. Do you:

A   Give up the idea of the class, even though you feel disappointed.
B   Explain about the class, and suggest you come to a compromise, such as him collecting you after the class.
C   Tell him it's your turn, and you are definitely having the car this time.
D   You don't even discuss it, you have already told him about the class.

8   You are conducting a business deal that involves selling a hundred items of your most expensive product at a discount price. This is still a good price for you, because the item has been slow to shift. Then, at the very last minute, your client calls and says they have a financial crisis and they can only afford to pay you 60% of the agreed price. Do you:

A   Agree to sell them the product at the price they say they can afford.
B   Negotiate a new price with them – for example, you split the difference.
C   Offer to negotiate on the cost of postage, but say that this is your best price.
D   Say the deal is off unless they can send you the amount agreed.

9   You are making arrangements to go on holiday with a group of friends. You are discussing the dates, and it becomes clear that everyone else wants to go a few days earlier than you would like to. Do you:

A   Find out when everyone else is free, and fit in with them, even though this means missing a couple of very important appointments.

- B 'Um and ah' about missing your appointments, but eventually go along with everyone else.
- C Ask the group to help solve this problem with you, and come up with a compromise that you are happy with that means you don't have to miss your appointments.
- D Say you are not going on the trip if you have to miss your appointments.

Scores

Your 'No' score: A's _____ B's _____ C's _____ D's _____

Mostly A's

Is there something about 'No' that you don't understand? You are diplomatic, yes, but this is always at your own expense. Other people can exploit you, and they do. Sometimes people find it difficult to respect someone who doesn't stand up for herself, and you are giving the message that you are a doormat.

What is it about saying 'No' that you are so afraid of? Why not identify just one or two current situations where you hate to say no, and ask a friend to help you brainstorm all the different ways in which you could give a firm and effective 'No' message. Choose the ones you feel least uncomfortable with, and try them out. Notice how you feel when you do it, and also notice the end result. Put yourself back in the driving seat!

Mostly B's

You are a great diplomat, and you hate to hurt other people's feelings. Sometimes you say 'Yes' when you really mean 'No', and this can give a confusing message. You tend to put other people's needs ahead of your own, and only think of your own needs later. Do you feel exploited or exhausted, and never have enough time for yourself? Does it make you resentful that other people seem to forget your needs? Do you need to be liked? Does this make you try to please others too much? Do you make promises and offers of help to other people that you don't follow through on? Have you considered making your own needs at least as important as everyone else's? Make time each week that is just for you, and make it clear that you have important things of your own that you must get on with. The issue for you may be about juggling conflicting demands, and your need to clarify your real priorities.

Mostly C's

You can say 'No' tactfully but firmly, and you can balance other people's needs alongside your own. You are not afraid to say no, and mean it, when you have to. You are capable of setting your own priorities and sticking to them, but this doesn't mean you are inflexible. 'No' does not cause you much stress because you have worked out your priorities and you are realistic about how much you can manage. You occasionally succumb to pressure, and resolve not to do it again, but generally you are able to communicate 'No' clearly and effectively, without unnecessary guilt or confusion.

Mostly D's

You live life on your terms. You have no difficulties saying 'No' and setting clear boundaries about what you find acceptable and unacceptable. This is something you learned to do a long time ago, and it is an essential part of your style that helps you stay focused and get things done your way. On the other hand, there is something about this style that suggests that at times you may be quite rigid about saying 'No' because you like to be the one in control most of the time. Your friends might give you a nickname like 'Chainsaw'. What would happen to you if occasionally you went along with another person's way of doing things?

Anxiety – what is it?

A small level of 'normal' anxiety - for example, concern that you will meet a deadline, which makes you work late a few nights to ensure you complete a job - can be helpful and motivating. But anything more than this, for example repeatedly worrying that you won't be able to meet the deadline, can be a drain on your health and create an unbalanced state of mind. A great many people who feel a bit under the weather are in fact experiencing symptoms of anxiety without realising it. Are you more anxious than you realise?

It is useful to understand what anxiety really is. Too much anxiety causes symptoms such as panic attacks or agoraphobia, a fear of going out or of meeting new people. It can make you restrict your life so that you don't have to expose yourself to the things that make you anxious. If you are not careful, this can mean you miss out on important opportunities. A lot of people with an anxiety problem live very quiet, restricted lives so they never have to face their fears, and they can continue to blame their anxieties and general low level of functioning on external causes.

Kelly is extremely anxious about flying. She tells everyone that she 'hates' flying and she closely follows airline accidents and disasters on the news, which reinforce her view that flying is really unsafe. Her brother, Mark, is interested in transportation and sometimes he quotes statistics proving that flying is in fact the safest form of transport. He also explains some of the causes of accidents, and how unlikely they are to happen. When he talks to her in this way she blanks off and appears not to follow his argument, and Mark has noticed that she appears unusually agitated, drinks heavily, and insists that his informed opinions are 'wrong' and she is right. He would love her to fly to Germany to visit him and his family for Christmas one year, but she insists that he and his family ought to 'come home for Christmas', even though they have been living in Germany for over ten tears. Every time this is discussed she brings out the story of how terrified she was during an episode of bad turbulence on a transatlantic flight. She was travelling alone for the first time, and she had a panic attack, and felt completely out of control. She thought she was going to die and ended up needing sedation. She was highly embarrassed about what the other passengers must have thought of her. She is determined to avoid repeating this experience at all costs, even if this means missing out on a family Christmas. Even the thought of going on a plane makes her uncomfortable. She believes the solution is to avoid flying altogether, then the unpleasant feelings will all go away for good.

In fact, if Kelly does avoid flying altogether, this will not fix her problem – because she may well start to experience the symptoms of anxiety in another area of life. For example, she may start to dislike travelling on trains, and start to avoid doing this as well. This is because she has given herself the message that her symptoms of anxiety have an objective external cause, and that therefore there is nothing that she can do about it except avoid the cause. Although this approach is understandable, in view of the level of her discomfort and terror, it does not work. The symptoms of anxiety are arising inside her, and are not 'caused' by flying but by her own fear. Kelly is actually afraid of her fear, and she has fixed this fear onto the experience of flying. She has never questioned her anger about her brother living in a different country, or why she felt so embarrassed in front of the other passengers.

If Kelly is ever brave enough to go for treatment, she will discover it is not necessary to restrict her life because of anxiety, but that everyone who suffers from anxiety needs help to get through it. Even if you don't suffer from panic attacks as severe as Kelly's, problems with anxiety are extremely common. Unfortunately, people are not taught the basics of understanding and managing anxiety at school, so that common symptoms such as panic attacks are not widely understood. Once you understand what anxiety is and how to handle it, you gain power and control and new opportunities can open up.

Understanding anxiety

Anxiety is fear by another name. If something frightens us, we get anxious. If the neighbours' dog threatens to eat you when you walk past, you start to feel a bit worried every time you leave the house. It's easy to see the reason for your anxiety, and you will probably not worry about it, as it makes sense to feel this way.

However, some people start to get feelings of anxiety when nothing obviously frightening has happened. Or they get stressed and anxious long after stressful events have occurred. This makes them feel there is something wrong with them.

Anxiety affects people in three ways: through physical symptoms; through mental and emotional symptoms; and through changes in behaviour.

So what is happening to you on a physical level when you feel anxious? Imagine you are in the following situation: it is a pleasant summer day and you are walking along the street feeling relaxed and happy, when you suddenly hear a car horn and a screech of brakes right behind you. A car has been driving the wrong way down the street – it is a one-way street, and you know that – but you have been walking down the middle in a bit of a daydream. Before you have time to think about what has happened, you run or jump as fast as possible out of the path of the car. You do this in a matter of seconds.

Only once you have insulted the driver and continued on your way to the coffee bar do you start to notice your physical reactions. The anxiety response in your brain has been switched on, and has prepared your body for immediate response to danger. You feel wobbly and need to sit down, and you desperately need to go to the toilet.

If you are in danger, such as being chased by a crocodile, your heart rate shoots up, so it can pump blood to your arms and legs more easily, as you need to move your arms and legs fast to get out of danger. To keep your heart beating at this faster rate, you need extra oxygen, so you breathe more quickly. Your muscles become tense and ready for action, and this makes you feel tight, shaky and tingly. Because your limbs need all the extra blood, blood is redirected away from your stomach, and this makes you feel sick or that you have butterflies in your stomach. Blood is also redirected away from your brain, and this can leave you feeling dizzy. As your heart is pumping blood around your body more quickly, your temperature increases, so that first you feel hot, then sweaty, and after that you may feel cold.

All of this happens to you because the anxiety response is there to protect you from danger – instantly. The usual explanation for this is that the ability to respond to danger quickly with either fight or flight has been selectively bred into our species to enable individuals to survive, and this is something we all inherit. We have the same way of responding to danger as our ancestors had many thousands of years ago, even though our lifestyles, and how we think about ourselves, look very different. When this kind of thing happens to you, it's not difficult to understand.

However, many people experience the fight or flight anxiety response *when there appears to be no real external danger*. You can experience a panic attack that appears to happen for no reason at all. Or you can find yourself incredibly wound up and anxious about things that really aren't that important. What you are experiencing is all the physical changes and discomfort of the fight or flight response, but you don't know why.

Do you have the physical symptoms of anxiety?

These vary from person to person but will include some, but not all, of the following. Do you have occasional or frequent episodes when you experience more than three of the following symptoms? (Don't include symptoms that are related to any other physical condition you may suffer from.) Many people who get these symptoms don't realise that they are suffering from anxiety or from panic attacks; they think they have a physical illness.

1. Dizziness or light-headedness ☐
2. Feeling shaky ☐
3. Feeling hot and sweaty for no apparent reason, and then feeling cold ☐
4. Feeling weak and unsteady ☐
5. Needing to go to the toilet more than usual ☐
6. Muscular tension, or tightness ☐
7. Rapid breathing ☐
8. Feeling tight across the chest ☐
9. Dry mouth ☐
10. Feeling nauseous ☐
11. Butterflies or a churning sensation in the stomach ☐
12. Tingling sensations ☐
13. Increased heart rate or palpitations. ☐

Score

Number of physical anxiety symptoms: _____

If you frequently have *more than two* of these symptoms and you are sure there is not an underlying health problem, they indicate you are suffering from anxiety. This may be a level of anxiety that you are used to and it may not bother you. However, if stressful events occur in your life, this may push you into an *anxiety spiral*. It is important to train your body to relax and to refuse to pay attention to any nagging negative thoughts.

The mental and emotional signs of anxiety

What do you think and feel when your body is producing the physical symptoms of the anxiety response? Unless you understand the process, it is likely you will feel out of control. People who repeatedly experience the anxiety response are often afraid there is something wrong with them. They may be afraid that they have a heart problem, that they are going to die, or that they are going crazy. These thoughts in themselves are frightening, and they can trigger the sequence of physical symptoms. You then worry that something really is seriously wrong with you, and you feel more and more anxious as the physical symptoms get worse. Before you know it you are having an unpleasant panic attack. Thus, anxious thoughts and fears may trigger the physical symptoms.

In addition to this, some people also have a specific phobia, such as a fear of vomiting, fear of flying insects, or a social phobia. These deep-seated fears produce all the unpleasant symptoms of anxiety. People suffering from phobias can feel out of control and unable to help themselves. They keep having the same fixed, negative thought that if they are exposed to the thing that upsets them, they will die. They are often strongly resistant to any advice or practical suggestions. Until they themselves understand what function the phobia is serving for them, they are unlikely to be able to let it go.

Pam doesn't enjoy being in very crowded rooms, such as at opening nights or crowded parties. A friend has invited her to a gallery opening. She has misgivings, but goes because she feels she should be able to deal with it and she doesn't want to let her friend down. But just before she arrives, while she is parking the car, she thinks, 'Suppose I can't cope, and everyone sees me panicking?' The moment she has this thought, her heart starts beating faster. She notices this straight away, and then starts to breathe a bit faster. She then has more frightening thoughts: 'Oh my God, I'm going to panic again.' She is scared of the anxiety itself, and she is getting caught up in an anxiety spiral.

TIME, STRESS, ANXIETY AND RELAXATION

Ends here with extreme anxiety symptoms or a full-blown panic attack

Feeling out of control

Feeling really bad

Distressed feelings

More negative thoughts

More discomfort

More physical symptoms

Uncomfortable feelings

Negative thoughts

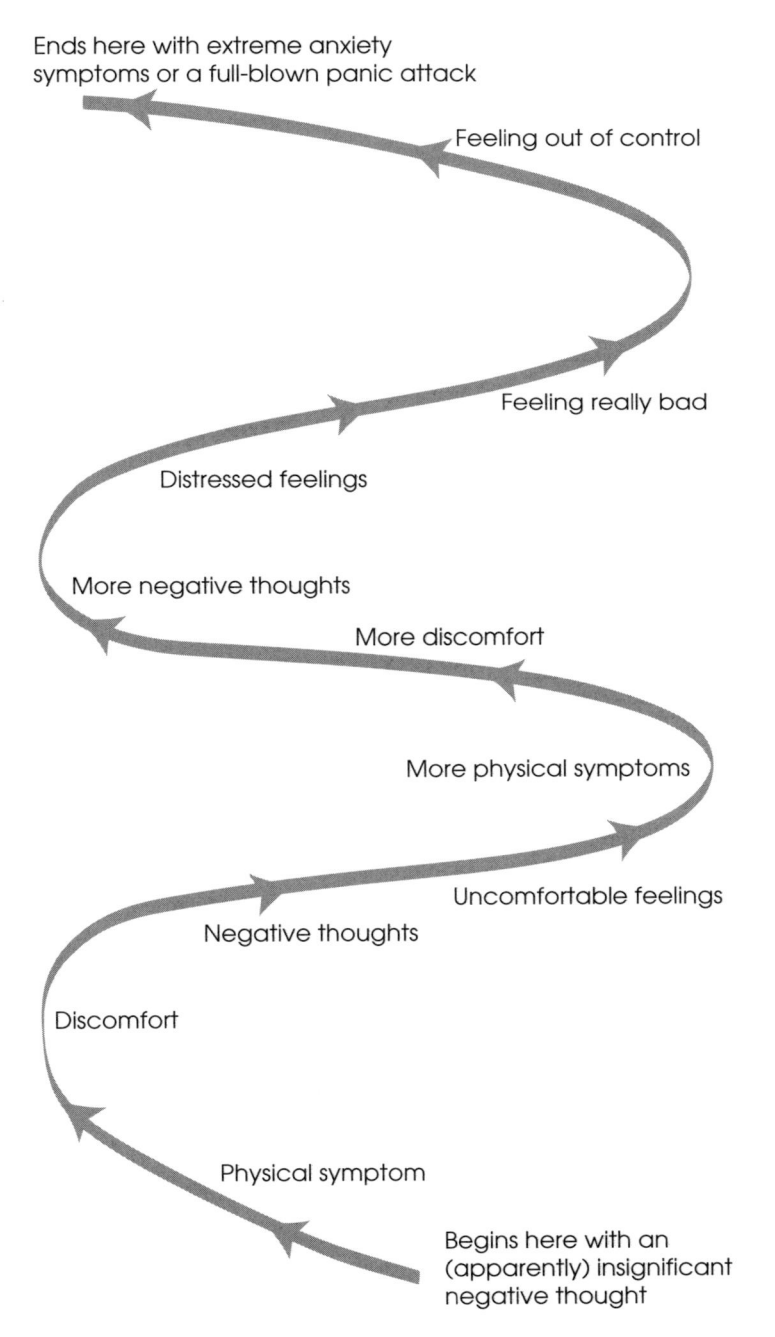

Discomfort

Physical symptom

Begins here with an (apparently) insignificant negative thought

The anxiety spiral: How anxiety and panic attacks are produced

Do you have the emotional and mental symptoms of anxiety?

We all have some mental anxiety. This is normal. It only becomes a problem when negative, undermining and anxiety-provoking thoughts start to reduce your quality of life on a regular basis, and you don't feel able to control this.

Add up the number of these symptoms that you experience

1. You suffer from intrusive worrying thoughts that you can't let go of.
2. You are a compulsive checker; for example, you worry about whether the back door is locked and check it several times before going to bed.
3. You are obsessive about washing or cleaning.
4. You need to be in complete control of your environment; for example, you won't let anyone make a mess in your kitchen.
5. You engage in 'worst case scenario' thinking; for example, you frequently fantasise about catastrophes or really bad things that might happen to you.
6. You have regular nightmares.
7. People say you are a pessimist, or that you always see the negative side of things.
8. Something is on your mind and is really bothering you.
9. You engage in 'global negative thinking'. This means you generalise, based on one experience. For example, it rains for a few days, so you tell yourself that it will rain all summer and you won't be able to do any walking, so you will get fat and unfit.
10. You are afraid of going out, or when you go out you usually feel the need to get back home as fast as possible.
11. You have a recognisable and specific phobia or fear – such as a fear of enclosed spaces, or fear of contamination – which substantially restricts you or reduces your quality of life on a regular basis.
12. You put energy into carefully avoiding the things that worry you rather than facing the challenge – for example, you are afraid of being in groups of people, so you have avoided going to college.
13. You have regular, intrusive self-critical or self-punishing thoughts such as 'I am fat/useless/stupid and I deserve to feel bad.'

14 If a sales assistant is rude or unhelpful, you dwell on it for days.
15 If you have an argument with someone, you feel bad for days.
16 You feel vulnerable or afraid that you can't cope on your own.
17 You worry too much about what other people will think of you.
18 You are frequently afraid you will lose control.
19 You frequently want to escape to a safe place, or go home.
20 You frequently tell yourself you are being stupid.
21 You try to blame someone else for how you feel.
22 You feel angry with someone else for making you feel this way.
23 You sometimes wonder if you are having a heart attack or a stroke.
24 You think that you are going crazy.
25 Your mind feels woolly and confused.

Score

Number of mental symptoms of anxiety: _____

If you have *four to six* of these symptoms, you can really relax! You generally manage to stay mentally calm even when provoked. You know that life is sometimes anxiety-provoking and stressful, but you know that the secret is in how you handle yourself. Perhaps other people think you are too laid-back at times, as if you 'can't be bothered' getting as wound up as they do. It's important to appreciate that having a relaxed frame of mind is healthy, and other people could learn from your example.

If you experience *six to twelve* of these symptoms on a regular basis, it is worth paying attention to your mental and emotional state. Do you sometimes slide into a habit of too much negative thinking? Remember to maintain a cheerful, positive and respectful attitude towards yourself. When negative thoughts and anxieties arise, remember to challenge yourself and take care to actively prevent them taking over your life.

If you have *more than fifteen*, your quality of life is being seriously reduced by these unpleasant symptoms. You need to challenge yourself to face some of your fears and make sure they don't prevent you having a life. Start with something small and build it up systematically. Would you consider some professional help such as counselling or an anxiety management programme? You should not accept or put up with these symptoms.

Do you have anxiety behaviour?

What do you do differently when you are anxious? Think about a situation that makes you feel anxious and how you handle it.

Often the single most harmful thing you may be doing which keeps your anxieties going is to try to reduce your exposure to your individual anxiety triggers. You avoid the situations that make you feel anxious. You feel that because you feel so anxious, the anxiety must be caused by the situation. In fact, this is giving in to your fear, and you then allow your fear to start making rules and dictating your life. Fear is a big bully that loves to make cowards out of us. The more we allow fear to rule our lives, the bigger it gets. But every time we decide to stand up to it, confront it, or even ignore it, the more our courage grows.

If you dislike going into busy supermarkets, you need to make sure you go shopping in supermarkets on a regular basis. By avoiding all supermarkets and buying your groceries in small local stores, or having them delivered, you never learn how to cope with your feelings of anxiety in the supermarket situation. You further reinforce the message to yourself that you are unable to cope. You may enlist friends and family to help you out – but if they do your shopping for you, they are not helping you to cope and do well, but helping you to withdraw from life. In effect they are agreeing that your fears are too much for you. Perhaps they would like you to be more dependent on them.

Anxiety can also be more subtle than this, and can be linked with self-esteem.

Claire is 29 and is fun, hard-working and attractive. She works in the finance industry as a consultant on investments and pensions. She is good at her job, as her clients enjoy her warm and friendly style, and she also gives them astute advice. She works hard for her clients, and keeps herself up to date with new products and developments. She is knowledgeable about the stock market and would love to work for a bigger company where there would be more opportunities to work with wealthier clients. A colleague tells her that a job is coming up that sounds really attractive – but when the job is advertised there will be competition for the post, and her colleague tells Claire that a man they both know is going to apply. Although he is younger than she and less experienced, he is dynamic and confident, and he is sure he will get the job. In fact he is already telling people that this is going to be his next career move.

Claire doesn't say anything. She goes home to think about it, and worries about whether or not she should apply for the job. She really hates job interviews, because they make her feel anxious and she is not good at selling herself. She feels people should be able to assess her ability based on her past performance, and that she shouldn't have to prove that she is good at what she does. She gets butterflies at the thought of having to sit in front of a panel of interviewers. Supposing she suddenly gets shy and her mind goes blank and she doesn't know what to say?

After discussing it with her boyfriend, Claire realises that feelings like this have held her back before, and that she won't lose out on anything if she applies for the job. Even if she does feel anxious about the interview, she doesn't want to use this as an excuse. She realises that she is the one who is holding herself back. She is also motivated by the idea of a higher salary with much better performance-related bonuses.

When she gets to the interview, Claire stays as calm as possible because she has prepared. She has had a yoga session and a massage the day before, and allowed herself plenty of time to prepare. She has written out notes of things she wants to remember to say, she has brought figures to demonstrate her track record with some of her clients, and does a persuasive presentation. She tells the interviewers that she is nervous and not good at interviews, but that she knows she is the right person for the job. She is careful to use her excellent interpersonal skills and to focus on the people in the room and what they want, rather than on her own anxieties. Claire gets the job because she is willing to make the effort to tackle her anxiety – and in so doing, all the effort she makes is worthwhile. The man who was confident he would get the job has not taken as much time to prepare, and this shows.

Do you really know how to relax?

Relaxation is at the core of a life free of distressing anxieties. If you take the time to learn to relax deeply, when stressful life events come along your base level of anxiety is low and you don't then get swept up into an anxiety spiral. If your base level of anxiety is always pretty high, when something challenging happens you are likely to find it much more difficult to cope than someone who makes an effort to practise being calm and centred. One of the reasons Claire got the job was that – in spite of her anxiety – she had worked hard to achieve a relaxed state of mind before going into the interview. Her yoga practice had helped her reach deep levels of relaxation on a regular basis. One of the reasons Claire had taken up yoga in the first place was that she realised she, her mother and her sister all had a tendency to be anxious and live on the edge of their nerves all the time. Every time a minor thing went wrong at home it was treated as though it was a major calamity. Claire found this exhausting. She really valued a feeling of peace of mind and harmony, and started to refuse to allow herself to be wound up. Her mother and sister perhaps slightly resented the way she seemed to become a bit detached from them, and accused her of wasting time 'doing nothing', but Claire started to feel better.

Sometimes people think they know how to relax – for example, they let go when they have a drink, they exercise or do gardening, and they sleep okay, so they don't consider they have a problem relaxing. They don't realise that not being able to sit still, having difficulty concentrating, or always having to be busy are symptoms of not knowing how to relax.

The relaxation questions

How many of these questions can you say 'Yes' to?

1. Do you engage in an activity specifically designed to help you relax? (This needs to be something that does not have any other major purpose but to help you relax.)
2. Have you ever trained in relaxation or meditation techniques?
3. Do you consciously take yourself into a relaxed state on a regular basis?
4. Do you deliberately work on feeling calm, centred and focused when life is stressful?
5. Do you have the time and space to completely relax from time to time without interruption?
6. Are you happy to spend time 'just' relaxing without having to do or achieve anything or be entertained? (For example, people are not in a state of relaxation when they are watching television; vegging out is not the same as deep relaxation. This is equally true for children, who can suffer from attention-deficit problems if they watch a lot of television.)

Score

How many relaxation questions did you say yes to?

Less than 2

It's likely you are not really on top of the relaxation idea. Maybe you don't see the point – but sooner or later, stress will affect you, and you have not built any reserves into your system. Learn to relax now before it becomes a serious issue.

2–4

You get the general picture, and you take time out to relax, but sometimes life takes over and you don't always give yourself the time you need. Remember that relaxation needs to be a priority if you are to feel your best, and refuse to allow other pressures to erode your relaxation time.

Over 4

You are well aware of the need to consciously relax, and you are good at taking care of yourself in this department. It's important you continue the good work! Don't let other people who are wound up and always on the go erode your peace of mind. Your peace of mind is precious and needs space and protection.

Press pause

A technique to help with the mental and emotional symptoms of any form of difficulty or stress.

1. Take note of what is on your mind that is bothering you. Take control of your breathing. Breathe, gently and calmly, into your belly. *Don't breathe rapidly into your chest.*

2. Ask yourself *how you feel* about the problem. Just *observe* how you feel – don't try to change it. If possible, notice where the feeling is located in your body. Notice exactly what it feels like, and also if it has a shape, colour, or name. Allow yourself to feel what you feel.

3. Ask yourself *what you think* about it. Just observe how you think. Then try to stop any thoughts that are negative and unhelpful by focusing on a constructive, positive thought. For example, if the thought is 'I'm afraid I'm going to die', tell yourself 'I know I will get through this'.

4. Resolve that you will take a few moments to yourself before you take any action. Keep breathing.

5. Do what needs to be done, *taking good care of yourself* and your needs during the process. Continue to observe how you feel and think while you work on achieving the outcome. Try to keep *a balance of attention in and out* – some attention on the problem situation, and some attention on yourself. Never give all of your attention to the problem itself, but always give some attention to observing yourself and how you are handling yourself.

Mindfulness

Mindfulness is a way to beat mental and emotional stress and improve your quality of life. It's a skill that is a combination of self-awareness, being in the present moment, and paying attention. It is taught in a variety of different meditation and relaxation classes. When you are mindful, you are relaxed yet alert and present. Mindfulness refers to having the right amount of attention engaged in something; enough effort to keep you focused and alert, but enough relaxation so that you are also calm and centred and you don't get completely caught up in whatever is going on. Your attention is balanced – you are giving attention to the stuff you are doing, but you are also giving some of your attention to yourself at the same time. You are aware of your state of mind, your feelings, and your body. (There are times when it is almost impossible to be mindful – when you are experiencing very strong emotions, pain or shock, for example. When you go into shock, freezing, or fight-or-flight mode, your body and mind are just fighting to survive.)

Another use of the word mindfulness means thoughtfulness or caring, for example caring about someone in a relationship, or being thoughtful about the assumptions you make, such as not agreeing with the majority view for the sake of it, but thinking it out independently.

Mindfulness training usually involves working with your breath as an anchor or focus for body-mind awareness. Simple yoga breathing exercises can be very helpful, such as breathing in for a count of three, holding your breath for a moment and then breathing out to a count of three. Breathe in through your nose, and out through your mouth. Breathe into your navel area and not into your chest, breathe gently and deeply, and don't breathe too hard. If you are not used to any kind of breathing exercise, it is best to start practising while lying down or sitting in a comfortable and relaxed position. It is possible that to begin with you could feel lightheaded, and if this happens all you need do is breathe a little less deeply. You can use this exercise all the time. It sounds simple, but it is highly effective if you remember to practise it throughout the day.

How mindful are you?
Take the mindfulness test

1. Is your attention scattered or do you have difficulty concentrating?
2. Do you feel at odds with yourself in a rather indefinable way or wish you were somewhere else?
3. Are you sometimes insensitive to your own needs, or do you ignore or override them?
4. Are you sometimes unaware of what is happening in the here and now in the world around you?
5. Do you tend to focus overly on achieving or reaching the end result rather than paying enough attention to the present experience and the processes you are engaged in?
6. Do you drive yourself through life at high speed most of the time? You don't care how you use yourself, you just want to get the job done, so that even if you are tired or hungry you won't give yourself a break.
7. Do you think relaxation, meditation or yoga are a waste of time or just for girls? You wouldn't practise some form of mindfulness-enhancing exercise or discipline on a regular basis.

Score
Number of mindfulness questions you said yes to: _____

If you said yes to *more than two*, you would benefit from some form of simple mindfulness practice. This can be as straightforward as remembering to breathe and centre yourself before you go into a stressful situation.

Recognising mindfulness
You can recognise when you are being mindful when:
- You feel that you are in flow and you are breathing rhythmically.
- You feel balanced and effective, involved but calm.
- You allow feelings and thoughts to surface into your awareness without suppressing them, but you don't let them distract you.
- You can focus on something, but you can take care of yourself at the same time.
- When necessary you can focus and concentrate without getting easily distracted.

Being mindful gives you a firm foundation for handling whatever life throws at you. It means you don't have to succumb to your anxieties and fears, and you can work through the long-term sources of stress in your life. Mindfulness means being a little bit detached from your everyday worries, knowing that inside yourself is a reserve of tranquillity that is not threatened by all the stuff that happens on the surface of life. This is like a deep pool of water being stirred up by the wind. The surface layers are ruffled, but the water deep down in the centre remains calm and clear.

A visualisation exercise

Some people find that visualising or imagining themselves in a pleasant, relaxing situation really helps them to relax deeply. If this works for you, your imagination can be a great resource. You can use the suggested visualisation below, or make up your own. Some people find it helpful to record it onto a tape in advance, so you don't have to worry about the details. You can also add your favourite soothing music to the tape.

This exercise is a fusion of traditional Buddhist mind-training techniques with contemporary relaxation training and visualisation techniques.

Visualisation

First make sure you are physically comfortable and that you are not going to be disturbed for twenty minutes to an hour, depending on the time you are able to set aside. You can also do this just before you go to sleep. Make sure you are not wearing any tight clothes, and that you are sitting or lying in a comfortable position with your back and legs straight and supported. It helps if you are in a quiet room with low lights.

Close your eyes, and begin to focus your attention on breathing. Just begin to notice the flow of breath coming in through your nose and pouring out through your mouth. Just observe your breathing for a few minutes. This is an exercise in focusing your attention and not letting it wander all over the place. If at any time throughout this exercise you become distracted, either by your own thoughts or by things happening outside the room, just bring your attention gently back to your breath. Practise letting go of all the different thoughts that emerge. Watch them go past, like trains leaving a station – but you are not going to jump on any of the trains, just watch them go by.

Whenever you get distracted, use your breath as the anchor to pull you back. This part of the exercise is important, as it sets up the basis of relaxation in both mind and body, so don't move on until you feel comfortable with it.

It is important to breathe steadily and gently into your belly area so that if you interlace your fingers just above your navel you can feel them move apart slightly as you breathe in. Allow the front of your body to soften as you do this, and don't breathe hard.

Now spend a few minutes scanning and observing how you feel in your body. Move your attention through your entire body, from the tips of your toes to the top of your head. Notice how your body feels. If you feel tense, you can also go through the process of tightening and then relaxing each muscle group as you go. Breathe in as you tighten up, and breathe out as you let go. If you notice any areas that are uncomfortable, aching, sore or tight, spend a bit of extra time just breathing in to these places. Breathe in a sense of peacefulness and well-being; breathe out your old tensions, worries and anxieties. You can also visualise breathing in a warm, energising red light that starts to fill and warm you with each breath. Allow this warm red energy light to make you feel confident, relaxed and peaceful.

Now move your attention to your thoughts and feelings. As you continue with your breathing practice, just notice the kinds of thoughts and feelings you are having today. Whatever state of mind you may be in, don't get caught up in it too much. Just notice it, whatever it is – cloudy, confused, easily distracted, preoccupied, blank – there are all kinds of states of mind we habitually slip into – don't treat it too seriously. Just notice it, acknowledge that this is how things are today, and pay attention to your breathing practice. If any thoughts and feelings remain particularly insistent you can look at them later, but don't get caught up in them now.

Now, as you are breathing, bring your attention to your forehead, between your eyes, and in your mind's eye start to imagine that you are in a location that you really love and that makes you feel well, relaxed and happy. You can choose where – somewhere that you would really love to be right now.

Keep breathing, and notice the details of what it is like to be here. Notice the temperature, the sounds, the feeling of air or water on your skin, the colours, and all the things that are around you. Notice who, if anyone, is with you. Notice what you are wearing and how it feels. Allow yourself to really enjoy being here. This is a special energising and renewing place that is completely safe for you, and you can come back here whenever you choose.

You may choose to stay here where you are, or you can continue a bit further. If you want to continue, you find yourself moving towards a small hill or slope, on which there is a beautiful building that attracts you. As you walk along – if you are walking – feel the ground under your feet and remember to breathe.

As you come closer to the building, you realise that there is someone special here who is waiting to meet you. You go to the place where you will find this person or being. As you first catch sight of them, you realise that they have a message to give you. Spend time observing this person, and continue breathing. Allow yourself to move closer to them, and notice carefully the details of your greeting and any words you exchange. The person knows you have come to collect your message, so all you need do is ask and wait. Allow whatever comes, and receive it.

In your own time, you need to say goodbye and return to your starting point.

As you make the return journey, you can reflect on whatever was said or given to you, and you know that you can return whenever you need to.

Now you find yourself back where you started, peaceful and energised. Spend as much time here as you need to before you start to bring your attention down into your feet. You can wiggle your toes and stretch as you begin, very gently, to come back into the room. It is very important to make the transition gentle, and to bring the feeling of peaceful relaxation and well-being with you. Try breathing in the thought, 'I feel well and happy.' Keep breathing as you become aware of your body here in the room; notice the sounds around you, and how you feel about coming back. Only open your eyes when you feel ready. Make sure you take care of yourself until you are fully present in the here and now. Don't immediately move into something busy or stressful, but allow yourself time to relax.

When you first try this exercise you may find it sends you to sleep. This is fine if it is what you need, but again be gentle with yourself when you wake up. Try to connect with the breathing practice and the sense of relaxation in your everyday life; make space for them rather than thinking you can't allow yourself to feel peaceful because you have so much to do. Give more space and attention to your sense of well-being and peace, and it will grow.

chapter 4
dealing with the past

'The past is never dead. It is not even past.'

– William Faulkner

Is a part of you still living in the past? Are you conditioned to respond to current situations by the way things happened before? Unfortunately, the past doesn't just go away when you want to forget about it. The truth is that we never forget anything that has happened to us; even though we may not have direct access to those experiences and memories any more, we store them within us.

The contents of this chapter may not look cheerful – being stuck in the past, being depressed and coping with unresolved grief – but as a psychotherapist I have found that people experience a great deal of relief when they have the tools to unstick themselves from the past. Denying or simply not realising that we are stuck is what keeps us firmly in the same place. Facing it opens up new possibilities of change, adventure and optimism. Some people think of others who are stuck in the past as 'self-indulgent': bad stuff happened, so they refuse to stop sulking until everyone apologises and turns over a new leaf. I prefer to view this type of self-indulgence as not knowing what else to do, and feeling hurt, angry, revengeful or traumatised. No one can move on when strong feelings like this are blocking their way.

Are you living in the past?

Before you read on, try this introductory questionnaire.

1 How often do you find yourself telling the same stories about things that happened in your early days?

A People's eyes glaze over and they listen politely but you carry on regardless.
B You tell stories sometimes, when it illustrates something that you want to say.
C Sometimes people ask about your past, but you prefer to avoid going into it.
D You sometimes discuss your past when it seems relevant.

2 Do you find yourself complaining about how much the price of things has gone up since you were younger?

A Frequently.
B Sometimes.
C You can't really remember how much things used to cost.
D Hardly ever.

3 Many years ago, you lost a beloved pet.

A You have never got another one, as you couldn't face the pain of losing it.
B You may have had pets since, but they have never been the same.
C You never got another one as you lost interest in pets.
D You have had pets since, and have loved them all as much.

4 Do you like to try out new things such as foods, fashions, travel or experiences?

A You prefer to stick to what you know and like.
B Sometimes you try new things out.
C You are not attached to any special foods, products or experiences, you take whatever's going.
D You are wide-ranging, curious and adventurous in your tastes.

DEALING WITH THE PAST

5 Your maths teacher told you that you were useless at maths and there was no point in continuing to teach you. How have you dealt with this?

A You believed what she said and have never taken it further.
B You have struggled with maths enough to get by.
C You have tried to avoid maths as much as possible, even though it has limited your options.
D You got somebody to teach you properly, so lack of numeracy skills never gets in your way.

6 Do you hold on to hurtful, damaging or negative things that people have said about you, or to you?

A You have a memory like an elephant; you never forget.
B You try to forget about them, but they sometimes come into your thoughts.
C Why should I bother about what they think?
D You go over things like that until you have sorted them out in your own mind.

7 How much do you like to learn, study and find out new information and areas of knowledge, or enhance your existing skills and knowledge?

A You rarely read books, go on courses or watch educational programmes – you prefer practical living.
B You like to read and watch things on television.
C You think formal learning is not relevant and is a waste of time.
D You are keen to learn and study, you take courses if you can, and you always have a book on the go.

8 How easily do you let in new information?

A People often say they have told you something you don't remember, or that you don't listen when they try to tell you something.
B Sometimes you find taking in new information can be overwhelming.

C You are not always interested enough to bother.
D You enjoy taking in new ideas and challenging yourself with new information to process.

9 How much do you live in the present moment?

A You often find yourself daydreaming about the past or planning ahead.
B You live in the present, but you also think about the past quite a lot.
C You live in the present; what's gone is gone.
D You try to live in the present, but learn some specific lessons from the past.

10 How forgetful are you?

A Your long-term memory is much better than your short-term memory; you tend to forget some everyday details or information.
B You seem to remember some things and forget others.
C You have a hard job keeping track of information if you don't write things down and keep organised.
D You seem to remember the things that are important.

11 Do you sometimes think that you find yourself in the same situations or having to face the same problems over and over in life?

A Yes, definitely.
B Yes, there are some things that keep happening again, without your intending them to.
C No. You try to move on, forget and never repeat the past.
D When this happens, you try to understand and work out what pattern you are repeating.

12 After you have been in a new relationship for a while, do you find that the person starts to remind you of previous partners?

A You have only ever had one serious relationship; or, yes, your partners have had marked similarities.
B You try to choose people who are different but sometimes they are more similar than you first thought.
C Everyone is different.
D Some things are different, and some things are the same; you try to understand what is driving your choices.

Scores

Add up the number of answers you have in each category:
A's _____ B's _____ C's _____ D's _____

How much are you living in the past? Very few people will score answers in just one category; read the comments for each category in which you had two or more answers.

A's

People who score strong A's are those who have been through some significant experiences in their early life that, for whatever reason, they have not been able to fully process. For example, you may have relocated and left an old life behind, there were losses or difficulties that no one talked about or that you couldn't deal with at the time, or you had to cope with things on your own when you were still young. You may be conservative in your views, and you may resist change and new information because you can find this uncomfortable or threatening. You may not like your beliefs to be challenged. When you feel secure, you are able to embrace change, but you don't like things to be forced on you.

B's

You may be living in the past more than you realise. It can creep in and distract you. Perhaps there are things from the past that deserve your full attention and understanding. Have you distracted yourself from them, numbed out or avoided them over the years, or told yourself not to be so silly and to just get on with it? You are not as logical as you would like to be, and are affected by emotions that you cannot control. Give yourself more space to explore your real thoughts and feelings, and you may find that things can work out differently.

C's
You have quite a fixed attitude towards the past: what's gone is gone and you don't want to indulge in it. However, a lot of your energy is being used up in keeping the past at bay and preventing it from affecting you. This prevents you taking in new information and adapting to change, and you can be intolerant of anything that threatens your carefully balanced status quo. The past will not kill you now if you do let it catch up with you, and you might be able to relax about it.

D's
You are insightful and aware of the effects of the past in your life. You try to learn from past experience, and are interested in dealing with any repeating patterns that you become aware of. You are aware of your history and how it has made you who you are – this is known as 'biographical competence'. You have a sense of where you came from, and this helps you clarify where you are going. You are able to make new choices because you are fully aware of the choices you made in the past, and why.

Time line

Develop your biographical competence, and fill in the time line of your life (opposite). This is like a visual c.v., but rather than focusing on your career it focuses on all aspects of your life. On the line, mark all the significant events, relationships, places, achievements, losses, memories and dates that you can think of. Focus particularly on all those times of transition – leaving primary school, leaving home, going to college, leaving college, your first serious relationship, etc. Use a vertical line for each event, with a descriptive text leading off from it. Try to complete the whole story of your life up to the present day. You can also look at the possible branches it might take in the future to complete the picture.

Your time line

Surviving the past

What do you think about the saying 'When the going gets tough, the tough get going'? Or the philosopher Nietzsche's remark that 'What does not kill me makes me stronger'?

This is one approach to handling the pain of change and disruption. Life is a series of phases that are ended by big disruptions. These disruptions are a natural part of the life cycle; for example, growing up and leaving home, having children, reaching mid-life, coping with the big challenges that everyone has to face. Each disruption breaks apart the old and brings in the new. At these times people fall apart and disintegrate so that they can expand to accommodate and integrate the new reality. Sometimes people temporarily break down under the strain, or become ill. This process of change is intrinsically painful; as a result we wish time would stand still and nothing would change, and that things would stop going wrong. But in fact there is nothing wrong with this process of change, except our own dislike and resistance to it. We survive. And more than survive, we grow, change and develop as human beings. We become more complex, we develop more skills, abilities, sensitivity and understanding; we become more patient and insightful. Think about all the cataclysmic events you have already survived – ever since you left childhood. What are some of the things you have learned from all this?

Our continued growth and development depends on our ability to fully experience everything that has happened in our lives – neither feeling defeated by nor avoiding this experience. Growth occurs when a person can make sense out of what has happened to them by facing it honestly and working things out internally. This enables you to develop a sense of competence and trust that you will be able to handle what life throws at you. We need hope, a sense of humour, good companionship and some self-discipline to support us on our forward journey.

What special abilities, insights and skills has your past given you?

1.

2.

3.

4.

5.

6.

7.

8.

9.

10.

The transference trap

Transference is a phenomenon that occurs in all relationships. It is what happens when we experience another person we are relating to in the present through the lens of our past experience. Most of the time we don't notice it, but in close relationships transference becomes much more intense. It can mean you don't hear what someone says, but what you think they have said, which is subtly different. What you think they have said is to do with your own history and expectations. On a subtle level we can 'expect' someone to behave in the same way as someone else did in the past. Their behaviour can look identical to us, even though it is not. These kinds of misunderstandings in communication create arguments and unhappiness.

Expectations built on the past are a cause of general negativity: you were let down and lonely in the past, therefore the future will be lonely too, just the way it has always been, and you don't really believe anyone who says they want to stay around. This is where the idea of the 'self-fulfilling prophecy' came from.

Joanne's boyfriend asks her if she can take the garbage out. He is busy fiddling with the remote control for the television set. Joanne's first response is to feel angry. She is outraged – how can he just sit there on the couch and boss her about like that. Then she feels fed up – she always takes the garbage out, and he hardly ever helps with anything. She works full-time as well as taking a college course, but he assumes that she has got nothing to do in the evenings but clean up after him.

Joanne is 33 and still living out a story that she learned from her parents. They didn't have a great deal of money, but they worked hard so that Joanne and her sister Laura could have the things they needed and get a good education. Joanne and Laura had music lessons, and they both had the things they wanted and asked for. Laura went to music college, while Joanne rebelled against her parents' expectations that she should do well, and instead of moving towards a career when she left school she travelled to India and moved between various jobs and boyfriends for some years. Joanne remembered the early years of her parents' marriage – she felt her mother was always working hard and making sacrifices for them, while her father used to come home, sit in front of the television set and wait for his dinner to be served. He would ask for drinks to be brought to him, and he never seemed to help around the house.

Joanne remembers him nagging her to help her mother, while he just sat there. She used to hate the way he made her mother work, and when she discovered feminism she was critical and negative towards her father for appearing so distant and passive.

When Joanne's boyfriend Steve asks her to take the garbage out, what she hears isn't just his simple request, but all the men in her history, starting with her father, who she feels have been lazy, exploitative and have taken the kind-heartedness of women for granted. She isn't going to put up with it. She tells Steve that he can take out the garbage himself, or get out.

Steve looks up from putting the new batteries into the remote control. He can't quite understand what she has said, or why she seems suddenly hostile, and asks her to say it again.

'You heard,' she says. 'I'm fed up with you telling me what to do. I put out the garbage every week – you never help me. I don't need you to tell me when to do it! You just sit there watching the bloody football all evening, I do all the shopping and cooking and cleaning up and you don't even ask if I want any help.'

'Hey,' says Steve, 'take it easy. All I did was remind you to take the garbage out – you asked me to remind you. I've fixed the remote control – it just needed new batteries, that's all. I thought we were going to watch that film you wanted?'

He has gone pale. He always feels terrible when she attacks him like this, and he can't work out what has gone wrong. He finds all this really stressful. His parents fought a lot when he was small, and they eventually split up.

If Steve and Joanne have enough foresight, they will seek help at this point, because the conflict they are entering into is too big for either of them to see clearly. Steve is experiencing something close to the catastrophic feelings he had when his mother insisted his father leave the family home. Joanne is re-experiencing the teenage rage she felt towards her father for bullying her mother – as she saw it at the time. Their reactions at this point could end the relationship if they are unable to step back and understand that their hostile feelings towards each other are nothing to do with the present. They are both trapped in the past and they don't even realise it – both of them think it is the other person's 'fault'.

It's not so easy to just forget the past and see things completely fresh. We all have a history of relationships, experiences and interactions that have helped to form and condition our personalities. But the past gets in the way of appreciating the present, and enjoying what we have now. Hanging onto the past is a persistent habit that is difficult to shift. There are a lot of self-help programmes which suggest ways of letting go and moving on. But how do you let go? It's not as easy as it sounds, because we hang on tenaciously to our sense of self. Even if life could be better, it's safe and familiar to be the way we have always been – and we simply don't know how to be different.

Letting go of old hurts and moving on is not the same as forgetting what happened. Forgetting, or 'I don't want to think/talk about it', is a way to avoid something that causes stress or pain. This ostrich tactic doesn't make it go away permanently. We can suppress or deny the impact of certain topics on us – or get irritable and touchy when other people bring them up – but these topics remain a dormant source of stress.

Joanne and Steve did manage to figure out what was happening to them, because they both talked about it with close friends, and one of Steve's old friends recognised that Steve was in a familiar pattern of feeling scared and demoralised in a relationship. Steve had been the youngest brother and was the most frightened by his parents' fights. He told Joanne how he felt when she shouted at him, and that he felt this was unfair. He felt he did pull his weight with sharing their joint responsibilities, but cooking and cleaning just wasn't his thing. In his family his mother had done all of that kind of work, and he had never felt confident in the kitchen. Joanne wasn't helping by confronting him in such an aggressive style.

Joanne cried a lot during this conversation, as it was addressing some really important and painful issues. They both realised that they did not have to keep re-enacting this drama. Joanne also realised for the first time – because her parents had never really explained – that her mother cared for her father when he came home because for years he was exhausted and suffering from ME. He had felt guilty about all the work his wife was doing, and this was why he tried to get his teenage daughters to help out. She realised that Steve was sensitive to her moods and found her confrontational style difficult to cope with. Joanne cared enough about Steve to stop making assumptions about his behaviour towards her, and he agreed to help more in the kitchen if she didn't criticise his failures so much. The conversation brought them closer together as they learned to understand each other better.

Difficult or uncomfortable memories

How do you know if you are stuck in the past? Do you process your life experiences so you can let them go eventually, or do you 'forget' about them so there is not the opportunity to re-examine them and put them in their right place? At any particular moment in our lives, we look at our past from a different point of view. If our view of any past life event is fixed and unchanging, it is because it is unexamined. If we integrate knowledge and understanding of the past, we are free to change and make new choices.

What about the stressful, painful or even traumatic memories in your life? These could be common everyday occurrences such as childhood losses and disappointments, an unhappy childhood, or difficulties getting established in life, or they could be really serious in terms of being traumatised, bereaved, neglected, abused or betrayed.

Difficult memories quiz

What are five of your most difficult memories? These can be from any period in your life. Don't think too long about it, just jot down the ones that come to mind.

1 _____

2 _____

3 _____

4 _____

5 _____

How do you feel about these memories now? Choose one of the following:

A It happened, I got over it, you can't live in the past.
B It happened, sometimes I still think about it, but it doesn't affect me in any way.
C Sometimes I still think about things and I can see they have affected the way I have lived my life and some of the choices I have made.
D I can't forget what happened, and I dwell on it almost every day.
E I still have nightmares or flashbacks; and/or I have persistent fears, such as phobias or serious difficulties going to certain places or doing certain things.

Scores

If you selected A or B, it means past experiences and relationships have left you with some unresolved issues. Even though you cope really well, these could be driving some of your behaviour and attitudes. This could be subtle and appear to have no connection with the original events. However, at times you may be defensive if certain topics come up. There are times when people close to you may experience your attitudes or behaviour as a bit erratic or awkward. It is as if you have not allowed the part of you that is still hanging on to these memories to grow up and be as mature as the rest of you.

If you selected C, you are a reflective person, and you know yourself quite well. This has been very useful to you, as you have learned to sort things out in your mind and put them in their right place over time. These insights could also make you helpful to others.

If you selected D, some of your memories are only partially resolved, and you would probably find it useful to speed this process up in some way so you don't have to keep carrying these uncomfortable experiences around with you. Life could improve a lot if you did this.

If you selected E, this is a clear indication that you need help with some past issues that are definitely not finished for you. Why not explore the options for what kind of help you think would be most useful to you? What has made you delay or avoid seeking help? The discomfort of facing past traumas and fears is never as bad as you think, as long as you choose someone to do it with who has the ability to support you appropriately. The worst things have already happened. Getting them out of the back of the closet and filing them neatly in the right order won't make them any worse.

The myth of moving on

Dealing with past memories, losses and change is not the same as forgetting the past and moving on as though nothing happened. Deep hurts flow from our past into the present, and healing and transcending them is a serious life task. Sometimes people think all they have to do is move on to the next thing, and avoid anything that has uncomfortable memories or resonances. Moving on is seen as the right thing to do. For example, they might feel that to live in a house that looks a bit like the one their parents lived in would somehow drag them back into the feelings of childhood. Or somebody gave them lemonade when they were a child and they hated it, and now they hate everything that has even a hint of lemon and go to great lengths to remove lemon from any food they are served. Avoiding lemons is avoiding the real issue – which is, *how is that memory still allowed to have such a strong effect on you?*

Memories like this are known to psychotherapists as 'screen memories'. This is a type of memory that stands in for a whole set of feelings, resonances and further memories to do with experiences that have not been fully processed and understood. These experiences have not been reflected on and digested. They 'just happened'. They are things we have swallowed and which are still running around inside our system because we have been unable to metabolise them. Memories like this need our patient attention and understanding; they need us to reflect on them and consider how they have affected us. If we can do this, our life experiences become a source of personal strength.

Rethink the past

We all hold some core beliefs from way back in the past which affect our self-esteem and confidence in some situations. These are not things we consciously think about, but they are things we have told ourselves as a result of experiences we have been through or what adults told us when we were kids. Part of the problem with these hidden core beliefs is that we don't fully realise they are there. They are truly hidden. Only someone who knows you well would ever guess they are there, and you yourself may never realise how faithful you are to the old way of seeing things. Another problem with these beliefs is that they are antiques. They are relics. They were invented by you when you were a child, or when you were much younger, when you had a more limited view of the world. They were decisions you made about how to handle life. They saved you from having to face each new situation from a fresh point of view, and now they actively prevent you from learning how to solve problems for yourself. They are no help to you as an adult in your complex, multi-layered adult reality.

Do you have core beliefs that began in the past that you think will never change? Did you receive childhood messages that you were bad, naughty, ugly, fat, not the clever one, not the pretty one, unpopular or unwanted?

Negative life statements

Do you secretly, deep down in your darkest moments, think any of these thoughts about yourself?
- 'No one loves me.'
- 'I must always be good.'
- 'There's no point in trying.'
- 'I am always the one who leaves/gets left.'
- 'Nothing I do will ever be a success.'
- 'I don't deserve to have what I really want.'
- 'I don't have any close friends.'
- 'Nobody loves me.'
- 'I don't have a right to be myself.'
- 'I'll never get the attention I need.'
- 'I always have to be nice and look after others to make them love me.'
- 'There's no point trying because I'm dumb.'
- 'Other people always do better/have more than me.'
- 'I'll never have what I want.'
- 'I can't trust anyone.'
- 'I have to do everything myself.'
- 'I must always look nice and be seductive to get any attention I need.'
- 'Everything works out badly in the end.'
- 'I'm no good at …'
- 'I'll try, but I'll probably fail.'
- 'I'll never have enough money.'

- 'I won't survive.'
- 'I'm useless.'

These life statements dictate some of our attitudes and behaviour if we don't realise that they are trying to run the show. They are trying to protect us – from too much risk, excitement or potential disappointment or failure. They also prevent us making whole-hearted new investments – in ourselves, our skills and talents, and in exciting new projects and relationships. They prevent us reaching for happiness, fulfilment and success.

Find out your negative life statements. Although it might be uncomfortable, you could ask someone close to you if they have noticed any tendency you have to be over-cautious because of negative beliefs about yourself. They might have noticed things you say frequently, such as that you are 'too tired', you 'can't cope' or you 'wouldn't be able' to do something. Discovering your negative life statements is very empowering. Once you realise what they are, they begin to lose their hold over you. Start to notice the negative things you say to yourself.

Identify and rewrite your negative life statements

Write your own negative life statements here

_____
_____
_____
_____
_____
_____
_____
_____
_____
_____
_____
_____
_____
_____
_____

It's important to translate negative life statements into positive ones, and to recondition your mind into believing something more helpful. Any beliefs you hold about yourself need to be:

- Useful
- Practical
- Realistic
- Constructive
- Positive

If you don't believe in yourself, who will? You can't get far without some positive life statements. People who refuse to believe in themselves are often difficult to be with. Believing in yourself is the bottom line for successful relationships and general success and happiness.

Translate your self-limiting beliefs

Take one or two of your negative life statements, and rewrite them into a positive statement about yourself. For example, if one of your statements is 'I always end up coping with difficult stuff on my own,' you could write, 'There are lots of people I can ask for help and support whenever I feel like it.' If a negative core belief is, 'I'll never have a nice home of my own,' you could write, 'Having a lovely home is a priority for me and I'm going to work really hard to make it happen.'

Positive life statements are really important, so take your time to come up with statements that feel really good, constructive and helpful.

Your positive life statements

1
2
3
4
5

DEALING WITH THE PAST

Being stuck

We all get stuck at times. This is when you can't seem to move forwards, as if invisible forces are pushing you backwards. Every time you make a big effort to move forward something else happens to set you back. There are times when it's best to ride with it, because you can't push the river. Sometimes doing nothing is very intelligent, because that way you don't make the situation worse. But sometimes you need to do *something different* to get out of the rut and move on. Does it take more effort, in the end, to stay in a rut or to break out of it? It all depends on your situation.

> Think about a time in the past when you were stuck, and you managed to break out and move on.
> What helped you take action?
> What would help you to decide to take action now?

'Every exit is an entrance somewhere.'

– Tom Stoppard, playwright

Rutbreakers

Rutbreakers are simple things that help you get a move on when you are stalled. Everyone has special favourites – here are a few that often help.

- Change location. Just go somewhere different, either somewhere you have never been, or somewhere you are confident you always feel good. If you can't move house, go on holiday. If you can't go on holiday, get away for a weekend. If you can't get away for a weekend, make sure you do something *new* and *different*, for example something that challenges you or makes you learn new skills. You don't feel like it? That is the whole point.
- Clean and tidy something. Not the whole house, but make one area, even a small area, fresh, bright and organised. Arrange some of your favourite things there, or get new ones. Then make sure you use the space for new and enjoyable activities, dreaming or planning. This is like feng shui for your mind.
- Throw out some old clobber.

- Do two or three difficult or tedious things that you have been putting off – just one or two a day. Just do it, but don't do too much at once. Just take one letter to the post office.
- Practise random acts of kindness. Give someone something or help them out. This is purely for selfish reasons – to help you feel better.
- Smile – there is research that shows that people who smile a lot feel better on the inside.
- Get some laughter therapy, such as the funniest movies you can find. If your life situation was a comic script, how would it go?
- Talk about your situation with someone who you feel is definitely not stuck at the moment – not someone who is, who will maybe sympathise with you and encourage you to keep her company. Try talking to several men about it – they are more likely to suggest solutions, and less likely to be sympathetic to your reasons for staying stuck.
- Try surrounding yourself with inspiring and uplifting music and fragrances, or aromas you totally love. They work for some people; 'Wake up and smell the coffee.'
- Definitely try exercising more, especially outdoors if you can, unless you are already devoted to daily sessions in the gym.
- Take a risk. Do something difficult. Take on something more. Challenge yourself even more. Achieve something that will astound people. This takes some of the pain away from the other difficult things and stretches your sense of competence.
- Change the paradigm. This means getting creative and redefining the problem. It's about finding a fresh point of view to look at it from. Write out your problem in the first person, in your 'I' voice. Then change to using 'he' or 'she' and write it from the point of view of a completely different person to yourself. For example, if you are a 32-year-old single woman living in the city, write your story from the point of view of a 55-year-old married fireman living in a country town. Does this sound ridiculous? He would almost certainly look at your life and your problems in a completely different way to you.
- Think about a time when you reached a dead end in your life. What was it like to get back on track? How did this feel? How did you regain a sense of direction?
- What is it that you would really love to do that you are not doing?
- Think about the things that really frustrated you as a child.

How did you deal with them? Is there anything similar about how you deal with frustrations now? Could you deal with them differently?
- What circumstances enable you to really feel at your best?
- Best of all, invent some creative rutbreakers of your own.

Depression

Are you depressed?
Depression is one of the main reasons why people get stuck in the past. Many people are depressed for a time without even realising it. One in four or five adults suffers from depression at some point in their lives; this seems to be true across most countries and cultures, although the figures may be higher in urban areas. A lot of people are depressed and don't realise it. It is a reason why a lot of people feel stuck and unable to move on. Depression is now being recognised as a serious disease of our time, with millions of sufferers in every country, and yet it is frequently unrecognised, undiagnosed and untreated. It is still something that can be embarrassing to admit to, as though to be depressed is some kind of failure. It is most common among those aged between 25 and 44, and at its most severe it can lead to self-neglect and self-harm, and sometimes suicide. Slightly more women than men are diagnosed with depression.

Depression can be about getting bogged down in stuff from the past, and not being able to free yourself. Everywhere you go, this old black stuff sticks onto you. Depression is a dangerous condition because it erodes optimism and hope, and makes people feel passive, powerless and unable to take effective action to improve things. Staying in bed, refusing help and feeling hopeless can seem like the only possible option.

Depression erodes your motivation and strength from within. You appear apathetic and to be your own worst enemy, and your family often lose patience with you. You lose all sense of ambition or desire, and just getting through the days and nights is all you can manage. You feel inadequate and underestimate your capabilities, and you may have to work harder to compensate for this. You feel slow and don't want to move or exercise. People tell you to get on with life, act cheerful, and stop bothering them with your gloomy attitude.

Depression is in fact normal. It is a perfectly logical response to difficult conditions in your life. It makes sense to give up when every door you try to open seems to be closed. Being depressed is a sign that you have reached a dead end. You can't move forward, because the way you thought you were going doesn't work any more. Depression is a response to difficulty, and this can come from within or without. Many people become depressed because of negative events, for example losing a job or a serious illness. But sometimes people can become depressed for no visible external reason, because they have a life-long tendency to have low moods, to be highly introspective, feel isolated or be self-critical.

We get depressed for all kinds of different reasons. Having to face loss and change, illness or disability, or that you are different in some way. Finding yourself unfulfilled, and without the opportunities to strike out in a new direction. Being stuck in a situation or a relationship that you can't leave because of responsibilities and commitments. Living life for other people instead of for yourself, or living by other people's rules instead of your own. Being isolated and not belonging to a community that gives you opportunities for high quality interaction and feedback. Even good news can make you temporarily depressed, because it might mean the end of an old, familiar way of life.

There are various different types of depression. Sometimes children are depressed because there is something they can't handle or manage, and it isn't recognised or understood that they need help. This can develop into episodes of depression as an adult. People who have experienced serious stressors in childhood, such as the loss of a parent or the family splitting up, are vulnerable to depression as adults. Sometimes people are depressed and there doesn't seem to be any kind of cause, but they may carry complex issues inside them that they are not able to understand.

In the end, only you can find your way out of it, and the best other people can do is offer you understanding and support and not judge you. They can cause more harm than good by trying to coax you out of it before you are ready, because this kind of getting over it is no more than window dressing, and doesn't address the underlying issues. The underlying cause is either that you are fighting to come to terms with something difficult that has happened, or that something central to your sense of identity isn't working in your life.

Pete is a car salesman who works for a big dealership. He has been the breadwinner for his family, and he has a thriving customer base. He is happy and successful, and he and his wife have three lovely daughters. There is, however, one thing that few of his friends or colleagues know anything about – he has secretly wanted to write poetry since he was about six years old. He distinctly remembers his father telling him one day not to be ridiculous, that no one makes a living writing poetry. He did what everyone wanted – and what a large part of him wanted – and become successful in his career and a great husband and father. Pete and his wife are materially comfortable, and everyone in the family is doing okay. The old desire to write poetry persistently nags at the back of his mind, and he tells himself it's childish and ridiculous. He writes a few poems from time to time but is too embarrassed to show them to anyone, even his wife. This becomes difficult when he secretly sends a poem in to a competition, and it wins second prize – even his wife had no knowledge that he had done this. He envies creative people, and has no idea how they achieve their success just by playing with words or music or paint rather than selling something real. In fact he has always been a bit critical of people who stay home and do creative things instead of working at a real job. Like his father, he has discouraged his daughters from 'wasting time' on non-vocational activities, and the family is achievement-oriented.

If Pete ignores his desire to write poetry for long enough, it will become a symptom. It will not leave him alone, and will make him ill. He will become depressed. This symptom of depression is there to force him to make the changes he needs to make so that he is expressing the neglected part of himself – in Pete's case this could be described as his 'inner poet'. What happens is that Pete starts to go downhill. He finds it hard to get up in the mornings, he can't be bothered to keep to his sales targets, he doesn't return calls, and he becomes grumpy and withdrawn at home. He wishes he could give up his job and go to university to study creative writing – but this is not a wish he could admit to anyone. His wife and daughters gradually adjust to him being withdrawn and carry on their busy lives without him. They think he is just in a bad mood, and they leave him to it. No one realises that Pete is slipping downhill fast, with nothing to hold onto. He starts to drink more.

You can stay in a psychic dead-end for years, and fulfil other people's desires for you extremely well – for example, you can play out the role of being a model husband and father, but never allow yourself time for your own interests. Your family might be happy for you to stay there, if it suits them. But this means you die gradually, you start to throw symptoms such as headaches or gut problems, you drink a lot, you distract yourself with all kinds of random enthusiasms or projects, you have affairs that end badly, you become irritable, anxious or withdrawn. You feel confused and lose self-confidence. You don't have a clear reason for getting out of bed.

Depression brings with it a dangerous opportunity. It says what you are doing or how you are living doesn't entirely suit you. It points out that there are unfulfilled longings or desires or conflicts of interest that you haven't admitted, perhaps even to yourself. Or else you are in a rut that is slowly killing you. It offers you an opportunity to do something radical to change this. There is some wisdom in it – it refuses to let you continue without acknowledging that you have a hidden problem of some kind that is calling out for your attention.

In Pete's case, his depression had a good outcome because he found a way to work with it. His wife, Lindy, thought that Pete must be stressed by his job and insisted he take some time off work. To do this he had to get a letter from his doctor, who saw immediately that he was low and not himself, and she suggested antidepressant medication. Pete was relieved in one way that she was treating his state of mind seriously, but the offer of medication brought him up short. He was not keen on taking medicines, even for a headache, and didn't like the idea that the medication could take control of his mind. The doctor accepted this, and then suggested counselling. Again, the idea of counselling made him feel uncomfortable. Counselling was just 'not me'. The doctor challenged him, suggesting that he needed to 'get things off his chest and not hold it all inside'. Who could he talk to? He thought about it, and felt he didn't really want to talk to anyone, but he could write things down. The doctor had been reading a journal article entitled 'Writing as therapy', and she agreed to let Pete go away and do this as long as he came back in a month to show her what he had been doing. She suggested a couple of books that were listed at the end of the article, under the heading 'Find your inner voice'.

The result was that Pete found he enjoyed doing the writing exercises. In fact, he enjoyed doing them so much that he couldn't stop, and he wrote so much it seemed he was addicted to it. Because it was justified in terms of 'therapy' and he was doing it for the sake of his long-suffering family, he didn't feel it was a self-indulgent waste of time as he would have done before. He literally wrote himself out of his depression, because writing was something he really loved to do and he had never before allowed himself the opportunity to really go into it. Eventually he found his way back into writing poetry, and decided to take an online poetry class to learn about techniques. Pete's wife and daughters were bemused by his transformation into an obsessive writer, but they accepted that it made him feel better. His youngest daughter, Lucy, encouraged by his new attitude, started to show him some stories she had been writing. Eventually Pete started to have more success with stories and poems he sent off. As long as he had time to do this, he felt more positive about his life.

The depression quiz

Here are twenty-six symptoms of depression. We all have some of them from time to time. We are all in a state of flux. You are only depressed if you have experienced *five or more of the following symptoms in the past three months.* Any one or two of these symptoms on their own does not indicate depression.

1. You have had to cope with bereavement, bad news, divorce or separation, moving house, loss, uncomfortable change or loss of health within the past three years.
2. You feel there isn't much you enjoy, or there is a lack of pleasure in things you used to enjoy.
3. You feel in a low, flat, miserable or gloomy mood for part of each day.
4. You are worse in the mornings.
5. You feel tired and heavy or lethargic no matter how much you rest.
6. You avoid all exercise.
7. You are over- or under-weight and feel unable to do anything about it, and/or you have no appetite, or you binge on mood-enhancing foods such as carbohydrates or chocolate.
8. You persistently drink, or binge drink, more than you know is good for you.
9. You spend a lot of time worrying, thinking or obsessing about your problems, and going round in circles.
10. You argue or resist when people give you advice, constructive suggestions or feedback.
11. You cry a lot.
12. You spend more than an hour a day watching television or engaging in other pursuits whose main function is to help you escape from how you feel in the present moment.
13. You don't take good care of yourself, for example your physical health or your appearance.
14. You procrastinate to the extent that you create problems.
15. You are aware, even if only in the back of your mind, of

something big that needs to change, but you don't feel able to tackle it.

16 You have a sense of an unfulfilled desire or dream, or a sense of something you are 'meant to do' that persistently weighs on your mind.

17 You stop yourself from having any passionate interests or joining in with activities you would love.

18 There is something you secretly long to do but you cannot allow yourself to do it.

19 You feel you have to live with a very big compromise, such as doing work you actively dislike instead of following a passionate interest.

20 You live, or work closely, with somebody who does not love or like you, or who doesn't treat you with respect.

21 Other people say that you are cynical, critical or negative.

22 You spend too much time alone, or lack enough close friends.

23 You frequently feel misunderstood, or different from most other people, in an uncomfortable way.

24 You avoid going out unless you really have to.

25 You feel trapped in your life circumstances and there is little or nothing you can do to help yourself.

26 You suffer from low confidence or self-worth, which inhibits you from doing things.

In addition, if your doctor has diagnosed you as being depressed and has given you antidepressant medication, there may be further clinically observable signs that you yourself may not be fully aware of.

Score
Number of questions you said yes to: _____

5–7
You may be suffering from mild to moderate depression. It is important to understand and assess the causes of this, to ensure that it does not continue. You may also need to give yourself a boost to help you get out of it. This could be something like a trip away, a change of environment or circumstances, or letting go of

something you know you don't want to keep hanging on to. If you feel you understand the causes, and you have the confidence to deal with them in time, then this is not serious.

7–12
It is likely that you are feeling moderately depressed, even though you may not realise this yourself. (Sometimes people get so used to it, they do not realise there is anything wrong.) It is very important to enlist some help, for example from your doctor, a good friend, or a well-chosen therapist, so that you begin to take action to confront your depression. If you ignore it, it will not go away.

Over 12
This is an indicator of moderate to severe depression. It is important that you start to face the issues that are preventing you from having a sense of self-fulfilment. There is a possibility that you are seriously depressed, and in some areas of your life you may have given up hope that things could get better. You would not be reading this if you did not have some hope, so it's important that you find someone who can help you take a fresh new look at things.

Tackle depression step by step

If you are depressed, here is the first thing to do to tackle it. Ask yourself what are five things you could do that would help you feel a little bit better – today, tomorrow, the day after tomorrow, and going on into next week. These need only be small things, such as making yourself a delicious meal, booking a massage, or arranging to meet a really good friend. They will be small steps, but these small steps are the beginning of a new journey.

The attitude of trying to help yourself out of your depression is what counts. You need a kind, patient, understanding attitude towards yourself. You do not need to be self-punishing, neglectful or self-critical – this never helps.

1 _____
_____

2 _____
_____

3 _____

4 _____

5 _____

Now check out the possibility of self-sabotage. Write down five reasons why you feel you can't, or may not be able to, carry out these suggestions over the next few days. When you have written these reasons down, have a good look at them. Who or what could help you get around these obstacles?

1 _____

2 _____

3 _____

4 _____

5 _____

Give yourself a break. You deserve to have a better, more fulfilling life, but unfortunately you are the only one who can take the first small steps to begin to make this happen.

What message is your depression giving you?

In psychotherapy, a symptom is often understood as holding the seeds of the cure. No one is depressed without a good reason. When snakes shed their skins, they are said to be withdrawn and irritable. The symptom of depression is a way of forcing you to slough off an old skin to reveal the fresh new life underneath. The depression says that you have to find a new way of doing things. Sometimes we secretly know this in some part of ourselves, but we are afraid to move on because of the change, stress and disruption involved.

Just supposing this were true for you, what would this mean? What dreams, desires or ambitions have you forsaken? How and why is it appropriate for you to be depressed? Have you been trying to kill off a part of your life? What is going to happen to you if you are not true to yourself and let other people make decisions for you or influence you, when they cannot know the unique story of your life?

Loss and grief

Depression is similar to grief in its manifestations – there are many symptoms that are common to both, such as feeling sad, flat, miserable, hopeless and lethargic. An important difference between grief and depression, however, is that in depression there is nearly always a chronic self-esteem issue that has not been addressed. Depressed people blame themselves. They have a low opinion of themselves and they consistently underestimate their abilities. A recently bereaved person will also blame themselves and feel guilty, for example feeling they should have done more for the person who has died, or that they could have prevented their death if only they had done something differently. But in bereavement, this is a temporary stage in the grief process, and the bereaved person usually develops a more realistic view over time.

The loss of someone we love is one of the most challenging experiences we ever have to face. Everyone deals with it differently, although some grief experts have defined a grief process that people go through in recognisable stages, such as denial, anger, guilt, acceptance and recovery. In fact, people are very individual in the way they handle grief, and there is no 'right' way to grieve or 'recover'. There are very few people who are equipped to give you really helpful advice about this, unless they have been through it themselves – and even then, their way may not be your way. Statements such as 'time heals' are worse than useless when you are in the midst of grief. However, talking with other people who have experienced a similar loss can be reassuring, if they have managed to survive in reasonably good shape.

Many people feel they should 'get over' the death of someone close or important, and that they are showing weakness if it still makes them upset and wobbly after a few years. Sometimes people are told to let the lost person go. This is unhelpful and unrealistic. Your relationship with that person, dead or alive, is an important part of you, and you can't just chop it – or them – out of your life simply because you don't see them any more. You need to retain your relationship with the dead person. They may be dead but your relationship is very much alive, and there is no need to kill yourself off as well by giving up on your own life. You need to maintain a continuing bond in your own way, so that you yourself can live fully. Living a half life because you have lost someone special is something to fight against.

Unrecognised and hidden grief

A great many people are suffering from symptoms of grief that go unrecognised. There is a problem living in a culture that values moving on, 'getting on with it', coping, and the avoidance of vulnerable feelings or the display of emotions. Grief, mourning and loss are not easily understood – except by the people who have to go through this devastating and painful experience. It means many people's grief goes unrecognised, and is not dealt with. It goes underground. It turns into all kinds of symptoms – which do not appear to have any connection with the situations that triggered them.

Unrecognised grief includes losses that have not been fully mourned, and long-term grief that is caused by a major loss. Any major loss has unforeseen and complex consequences for the person's sense of self and identity, which will be changed forever by the loss of relationship and opportunities.

Hidden grief also includes grief about losses that have not been properly identified or recognised. This includes losses like 'empty nest syndrome', which is the grief a parent suffers when children leave home, for example to go to university. The reasons why the young people have left are positive, they are moving forward in their lives, but their parents feel bereft. It is not just that the house is no longer filled with teenage chaos or that the parents feel lonely without them. The parents have to face a more internal loss, that of being a parent of a dependent young person. They are no longer needed on a daily basis. Part of the parent's identity has been built around being a parent, and for a while they may not know who they really are or what they are living for without the kids to care for. A time of recognition and mourning of this stage is necessary in order to create a new space where other activities, and a fresh sense of identity, can take root.

Another source of hidden grief is the loss of childhood. Even in really healthy and happy children, much is lost when they move out of childhood and on into their teenage years. You never have quite the same relationship with them again. Teenagers also feel this, feeling confused about whether they want the security of childhood, or to be free and independent.

Moira suffered from hidden grief when her 30-year-old daughter Jacqui had an abortion. Although she supported her daughter in her decision, and cared for her afterwards, Moira herself had private, unspoken regrets about the abortion. This was because it ended for her a private fantasy she had had about being a grandmother, and about having time to spend with grandchildren that she had not been able to manage with her own children. Jacqui's partner was not interested in having children, and they were both investing in a fast-paced lifestyle. The fact that Jacqui was horrified that she fell pregnant upset Moira, but she knew it would be unwise to give her own personal viewpoint. Moira then had to live with the unrecognised grief that she might never be a grandmother.

The nature of unrecognised or invisible grief means there are few people you can share it with. It is really grief over your own future: a future that you have either lost, or that has changed completely.

Are you suffering from unresolved or hidden grief?

How many of these questions can you say yes to?

1. Do you get touchy, hurt or angry quickly for apparently small or insignificant reasons; for example, someone accidentally walks right into you in the street and you lose your temper?

2. Do you cry easily, for example when reading or watching stories about other people that seemingly have no connection to you?

3. Do you sometimes feel overwhelmed by strong feelings that well up 'for no reason'?

4. Do you have feelings you feel you must hide, such as vulnerability or weepiness, for example?

5. Do you feel sad or uncomfortable around people who inadvertently remind you of someone you have lost? Do you avoid situations like this?

6. Do you reminisce or tell a lot of stories about the past, often telling the same stories even when people have heard them before?

7. Do you have a nagging sense of either regret or guilt that seems to be holding you back?

8. Do you withdraw into yourself or escape into a fantasy world almost every day?

9. Is it difficult to make constructive, optimistic plans for the future and to follow them through?

Score
Number of questions you said yes to: _____

1–3
Everyone has to deal with ongoing loss and change, and although this has affected you, you are aware of this and you are dealing with it as best you can. But don't forget to give yourself special

care and attention in this area. Don't ride over your sensitivities or tell yourself to stop being a wuss and get on with it. Listen to what your feelings are telling you in these situations. Are there things that you really need or long for? Do you need time to pay attention to your feelings and sort them out?

Over 3

You have suffered losses and setbacks, and it is possible you have not yet been able to come to terms with some of them. You may put a brave face on things, but are you trying to ignore some of your deeper feelings? Do you feel guilty or angry about stuff that happened? Do you believe that things can't get any better, or that you haven't got what it takes to make a new beginning? Are you in fact preventing yourself from moving on because the old losses or problems have still got hold of you?

Survival tips for grief

Coping with long-term grief is hard. It is important that you give yourself the help and support you need, and that you reach out to others as often as you need.

- It is very important to find benefits in your loss, and to realise what you have gained from it; people who do this regain a greater sense of well-being. They achieve greater mastery over their loss than people who feel victimised or entirely negative about the loss.
- Write the story of your loss. Confront the difficult feelings, and put them into words. Construct the entire story of the loss, and write a story that brings it all together. This process will bring up negative emotions, and initially it may make you feel worse. However, over time you will notice it has significant benefits. By allowing yourself to make a coherent story about the loss, you enable yourself to come to terms with it more.
- Talk about your loss, and make sure you have plenty of good social contact and are not socially isolated. Choose friends and partners who are empathic and easy to talk to.
- Give yourself regular times to reflect on your losses, so that you keep up to date with how you feel about them now.
- Give yourself time to feel the pain, so that it doesn't creep up on you unannounced.
- Keep a journal of your memories and dreams and your reflections about these; whenever a new memory comes up, give it time and space.
- Do something special and significant in your life which is a direct response or a statement about what has happened.
- Make a space in your home and your life where memories can be experienced and celebrated; for example, a special place where you keep some treasured possessions.
- Make sure you talk about people who have died, and don't let them be forgotten.
- Make something creative that expresses aspects of the lost person and your feelings and thoughts about them.
- Write or talk to them.
- Be patient; this is a life-long process and is never 'finished'.
- If you still feel guilty, get help with this as guilt can hold you up for years.

- Invest in new relationships and activities; use the opportunity to make positive changes and start again.
- Reaching out to others who have been through something similar can be helpful to you.

Post-traumatic stress

People who have been through traumatic experiences such as rape, violent assault, tornadoes or accidents can recover from the physical effects of the trauma fairly quickly. However, some people find it much harder to recover from the emotional and psychological effects, which can linger for months or years. People can develop a syndrome known as Post Traumatic Stress Disorder or Syndrome (PTSD). Many people have a mild version of this, and don't even realise they are suffering from it. Dealing with the symptoms of PTSD is very similar to dealing with the effects of loss. The person is traumatised, and needs to make sense out of what has happened to them. They need to face the difficult feelings, which might include sadness, despair, guilt, shame, anger, humiliation, helplessness or fear. It is important for them to be able to reconstruct the story of what happened, how they dealt with it at the time, and how they feel about it now. They need to regain a sense of control over their lives. They need to disclose and share the difficult feelings that they are left with, and they need to be able to talk with people who are empathic and understanding.

There is some evidence that PTSD can be worse if the person had disruptive life experiences prior to the traumatic incident, such as losses in childhood. If so, then these earlier events will also need to be revisited and included in the story of what has happened to them. If the person has people she or he can talk to closely after the event, this seems to be helpful. As with loss, it is empowering if the person can eventually find meaning in the incident, or some benefits in what they have learned from it. Going through a trauma results in a huge emotional upheaval. This makes people re-evaluate everything in their lives, and think differently about themselves. It can also make them feel very isolated, because they feel alone in the experience. Writing or talking about their story is essential in helping them to reorganise themselves and feel in touch with others.

'A thing which has not been understood inevitably reappears; like an unlaid ghost, it cannot rest until the mystery has been solved and the spell broken.'

– Sigmund Freud (1909)

As with loss, trauma asks for our skilful attention in order to heal. We need to mourn what happened to us, what we lost, and understand how we have changed as a result. Those who recover successfully from traumatic events seem to be those people best able to understand the events and their own response to them in a meaningful way. They can make what has happened meaningful to them.

How to recognise the symptoms of PTSD

- Do you have difficulty sleeping?
- Are you irritable?
- Do you have difficulty concentrating?
- Are you hyper-alert?
- Do you re-experience the traumatic event? For example, do you have distressing recurring dreams, flashbacks, or intrusive images?
- Do you experience physical or emotional distress when something reminds you of the event, even if indirectly?
- Do you avoid feelings, thoughts, people, activities, places or situations that remind you of the trauma?
- Are you unable to recall a significant aspect of the trauma?
- Have you reduced your range of interests and activities?
- Have you lost hope in the future?
- Have you become more detached?
- Has your range of emotional expression become more narrow and restricted?
- Have you developed any insistent repetitive thoughts or behaviours?

If you experience more than three of these symptoms on an on-going and persistent basis, and the symptoms emerged after you went through a traumatic event, it is a good idea for you to seek help. Everyone can experience these symptoms temporarily, but if they persist for months it means you need further help and support in order to recover.

chapter 5
happiness, joy and creativity

Happiness is good for you. Evidence from extensive research shows that having positive feelings and feeling good about yourself leads to greater creativity, better problem-solving, improved conflict resolution and more flexible thinking. Happy people are more generous and helpful to others, and their decision-making processes are more effective and thorough.

There are small things we can all do easily each day to gently lift our level of well-being and happiness, and therefore increase our effectiveness. We respond quickly to our surroundings and to small daily events that lift our mood – think how differently you feel if someone says something kind to you or offers you a small gift.

Joy goes deeper than the kind of happiness that fluctuates according to your circumstances. Joy is an inherent quality or gift that comes with being alive, and is not entirely dependent on external conditions. Thus we can still experience moments of joy even when we are having a bad time. To feel joy is a *human right* that is often neglected or underrated. We tend to feel we have to snatch a few crumbs from the table, rather than sit down and enjoy the whole banquet. Joy isn't something you have the time or capacity for if you are just surviving, struggling, getting along, managing pretty well. Or is it? Does joy have to depend on the things we have got, or is it a willingness to enter a joyous state of mind? Like pausing to smell the flowers as you pass by, to feel gratitude, and to appreciate the company of people you see every day and could take for granted. Who decides what we are allowed to enjoy and when we can do it?

Some of us grew up in a culture influenced by Calvinist or Puritan thinking. One of the central ideas from this philosophy, as it has been handed down through the generations, is that you have to work hard in order to deserve anything, and that joy, relaxation and pleasure for their own sake are frivolous, a waste of time, or self-indulgent – this is similar to the belief that sex should only be for the purposes of procreation rather than recreation.

Freedom

How often do you act freely and spontaneously, and do things that are not driven by worry or necessity? A spontaneous act of freedom is something that is not conditioned by fear, expectation or duty, but an act that is a form of creative self-expression. (I am not referring to acts of pure selfishness that inconvenience, upset or damage anyone else.) A personal move towards freedom requires courage and commitment; for example, taking the decision that you want to leave your lucrative but stressful career and retrain in a vocation that will give you a greater sense of purpose and inner satisfaction. Or taking a day off work – not to skive but because you really want to spend the day with someone special. Or doing or saying something unconventional and innovative, using lateral thinking or making a new suggestion that improves everyone's quality of life. What stops us occasionally taking this type of action is often our fear of stepping outside the boundaries of our self-built cage. We become closed-in creatures of habit.

The idea of the false self is popular in psychology. This suggests that there are two different types of upbringing. One is where the individual is moulded and shaped to 'do' and 'be' what is expected; as a result, the person develops a false, compliant self that meets external requirements, and gains acceptance, approval, a sense of fitting in and being the same as the people around him. Children who are only offered conditional love and acceptance – that is, they only feel truly loved if they meet certain imposed conditions such as 'Be nice' or 'Keep quiet and leave me alone' – can grow up feeling unlovable, and that they have to behave in certain ways to get the love and attention they need. They can feel empty and dead on the inside, and have low self-esteem and low expectations of life.

The other type of upbringing allows the child enough safely contained freedom from external demands to afford her space to play, fantasise and discover who she is. She is allowed space to explore and learn for herself, and comes to trust that even if some of her behaviour is unacceptable to adults, she is profoundly loved and lovable for who she is. Although a child brought up in this way will still learn to lie, adapt her behaviour to other people's expectations, and manipulate others to get what she wants, her false self is less central to her and does not determine her behaviour so much.

Maybe we all have a bit of a false self, in that we have to act a role some of the time. In the novel *War and Peace*, Tolstoy describes a man who experiences a lifetime of hardship, oppression and difficulties. What he eventually learns is that the most important thing is finding the personal freedom to make one's own life, in one's own way, and to love. The worst thing is going to happen to all of us: we are all going to die and nothing and nobody can change this. If we live with this in view, with the knowledge that we are going to run out of time, this can empower us to make the most of what we have here and now. The Existentialist philosophers regarded this as giving us the ultimate freedom: to make of our own life what we will.

Curiosity

Children come into the world primed to ask questions. They are explorers and adventurers. They are full of creative curiosity, and they want to know everything. In fact, research shows that babies are remarkably adept learners from the very first day they are born. Everything they manage and accomplish in their lives is based on the knowledge and skills that they gather. One researcher has suggested that children seek the answers to four basic questions:

- What's there? This is about exploring categories and concepts.
- What leads to what? This is about discovering sequences.
- What makes things happen? This is about discovering causes and effects.
- What can be controlled? This is about discovering mastery.

This natural curiosity is a great survival skill that enables children to understand their world and get the things they need. Why do we seek to restrict, or get bored by, children's questioning?

Joy

Joy includes happiness, pleasure, bliss and ecstasy. It is more than just pleasure, however; it is also your underlying capacity to choose and turn towards enjoyment, happiness or pleasure. Feeling joyful is an opportunity to fully experience an aspect of your own nature that is always already present. We choose people, activities and objects to enable us to experience and participate in bliss, ecstasy, pleasure and joy.

Each individual is a unique channel for joy and enjoyment, expressed through their relationships and their positive choice of external objects and activities of all kinds, which express their sense of self. This is easy to observe in people engaged in activities that create intense enjoyment and excitement, such as surfing or skiing, and the pleasure someone who loves these sports can take in a new surfboard or snowboard.

Growth and development are also accompanied by an increased capacity for enjoyment of life. Schutz, a radical psychologist writing in the 1970s, described joy as 'the feeling that comes from the fulfilment of my potential'. People who are more highly educated report greater feelings of fulfilment in later life than people who rejected education or training, as they are recognised and paid for their investment in acquiring wisdom, knowledge and skills.

If we spend enough time enjoying ourselves, we are less likely to be negative, envious or destructive. Why, then, is this considered to be a waste of time or self-indulgent? Why is it 'better' to do boring work than hang out doing something you love? One of the best things in life is to be fully absorbed in doing something you really love.

What is your joy rating?

Consider these questions carefully to gauge whether you are making enough space in your life for spontaneous joy and pleasure to arise. Tick all the questions you can say 'Yes' to.

1. Do you feel confident that you can cope within your current environment? ☐
2. Do you feel you can handle many different situations competently? ☐
3. Do you feel able to use a wide range of your capacities? ☐
4. Do you have opportunities to express your emotions freely? ☐
5. Do you have enough time for the things that matter most to you? ☐
6. Do you have a variety of positive and enriching relationships? ☐
7. Do you feel you participate in your wider community in a meaningful way? ☐
8. Do you find pleasure and enjoyment on a regular basis and make time to play? ☐
9. Do you feel some form of spiritual connection to life? ☐
10. Do you feel you are actively working towards personal, emotional or creative fulfilment? ☐

Score

Your joy rating out of 10: _____

What are things you can do to create more opportunities for joy in your life?

_____
_____
_____
_____
_____
_____

Are you unhappy?

Why do so many people feel unhappy and unfulfilled? Before we look at happiness, let's take a quick look at unhappiness. Some basic causes of this condition can be identified. If you can identity with any of the following causes of your unhappiness, you can – with some effort – change them completely. All of these factors can be changed once you recognise them for what they are.

1. Are you irrational? Do you base your decisions and everyday actions on illogical or unfounded reasons? Do your attitudes and beliefs weaken and undermine you?

2. Do you project your ideal version of reality onto people and events? (For example, you imagine that your new boyfriend or girlfriend is going to be your ideal life partner before you have got to know them properly; or you don't want to notice that your wonderful new business partner is cheating you.)

3. Is your life restricted by fear? Do you actively avoid pursuing your chosen values and goals, and do you live to actively avoid effort, change, disruption, loss or disappointment? Do any of these fears motivate you: fear of the new, fear of change, fear of the future, fear of difference, fear of judgement or criticism, fear of not belonging, fear of standing up for yourself, fear of success, failure or disappointment, fear of being wrong, fear of telling the truth, fear of loneliness, fear of effort or discipline, fear of discomfort?

4. Do you feel that making an effort to do something difficult is 'not worth it'? Do you live to expend the least possible effort in certain areas?

5. Do you fail to see that you can achieve and earn your own happiness through thinking, planning and pursuing your own values?

6. Do you have a low sense of your own efficacy and mastery? For example, if you experience setbacks, are you unlikely to persist? Do you give up easily?

7. Do you think of your moods and attitudes as being controlled by other people and external events?

8. Do you prefer to avoid problems that have to be solved and challenges that have to be met?

9. Do you have a pessimistic attitude about the possibility of getting what you really want?

Building blocks to happiness

Based on the new research in the happiness field, there are specific things that you can do to build your happiness, and specific things that you can do to reduce your chances of being happy. For example, the biggest single determinant of how happy people are as they get older is being in a good relationship. This would imply that it is worth making your relationships a high priority. Whether or not you are in an intense one-to-one partnership, positive human relationships are essential. In fact, strong relationship satisfaction can offset other factors in life that are linked to unhappiness, such as financial problems. The other strong predictor of happiness and well-being in later life is one's level of education. It seems that the more education you have, the more likely you are to experience a sense of purpose and of being fulfilled.

Supposing you were to decide to make happiness one of your main goals or desired outcomes within five years. Would you be willing to make the changes? Do you believe you can be happy, that you are entitled to a happy life? The questionnaire below is based on factors that have come up in a range of happiness research projects. These have shown that there are certain definable factors that influence people's reports of whether or not they feel they are happy. For example, money does make people happy to a certain degree. Being short of cash can make you unhappy. But once people have reached the point of affluence, increased wealth beyond this does not make them any happier. Feeling fulfilled, valued and able to contribute to your community or society seems to be much more clearly linked with happiness. People who have built up, and then sold, a successful business can feel bereft without it, and say that the money is no compensation for lacking a sense of value and purpose.

Answering these questions – some of which you may find quite thought-provoking – will also make you sit up and think about what makes people happy. In particular, what makes you as an individual happy and how can you get more of it? Some of the questions are not what you might immediately think of when you think of the word happiness. If you ask people what they think would make them happy, a lot of them will say 'Winning the lottery'. In fact, research done on lottery winners does not demonstrate that they are mostly any happier than the rest of us! You might find it fun to ask other people some of these questions, as well as yourself, and to carry out your own happiness research.

Happiness seems to be a combination of having acceptable life conditions and having a happy attitude. A happy attitude is in turn determined largely by your values and goals, and the behaviour that results from these. Happiness is to do with how you relate to your world. For example, some extremely poor people in third world countries report that they are very happy, because their level of poverty is normal, and it does not interfere with other aspects of their lives which influence how they perceive themselves, such as a rich social network or spiritual beliefs. They accept their situation and don't invest a lot of energy in wishing it were different. It is not accepting ourselves, our life or our situation that creates the most unhappiness, combined with a lack of positive goals. In fact, this may be the art of happiness: achieving a state of accepting what you have, while at the same time working towards increased fulfilment in the areas that you can.

HAPPINESS, JOY AND CREATIVITY

How happy are you?
The happiness questionnaire

Circle *one* number for each question, then total them at the end.

1   Money: do you have enough for all you need, and consequently you don't worry about money?

    | This is definitely true for me | 4 |
    | This is partly true for me | 3 |
    | This is not like me, but I am working towards earning more | 2 |
    | This is not like me at all | 1 |

2   Do you spend money on the lottery?

    | No, never | 3 |
    | Yes, occasionally | 2 |
    | Yes, every week | 0 |

3   Do you accept and feel happy with your situation in life?

    | Yes | 4 |
    | No | 0 |

4   Do you feel fulfilled in your everyday work or occupation, and feel that you are able to use a lot of your skills?

    | This is very much like me | 4 |
    | This is partly like me | 3 |
    | This is not like me | 2 |
    | This is not at all like me; I work to live, not live to work | 1 |

5   Do you have a relationship that helps you feel happy, with someone you can love and trust?

    | This is definitely true for me | 4 |
    | This is partly true for me | 3 |
    | This is not true for me but is something I would like to happen | 2 |
    | This is definitely not true for me | 0 |

6   Family: my family life (including children if you have them) is rich and rewarding; I love spending time with them.

This is entirely true for me	4
This is partly true for me	3
This is not true for me but I would like to make it happen	1
This is not true for me at all and I don't see how it could change	0

7 Friendship and support: I have a wide range of friends, some of whom are quite different from each other, and I actively maintain these relationships.

This is very much like me	4
This is quite a lot like me	3
This is not much like me; I have friends, but they consist of a small group of people	2
This is not me at all – I don't socialise or see many people	0

8 Education: my education so far has been fulfilling and helps me achieve my potential.

This is true for me, and I have invested a lot in my education	4
This is partly true for me	3
This is not like me	1
This is not me at all; I am not all that interested in education	0

9 Hobbies/non-professional activities/interests: I am actively involved in a range of activities, interests or hobbies that I enjoy and participate in.

This is very much like me	4
This is partly like me	3
This is not much like me	1
This is not like me at all; I don't have many outside interests	0

10 Is there something you do – it could be anything that doesn't cause harm and is not self-destructive – that gives you a real buzz and you wish you had more time for it?

Yes	2
No	0

11 Well-being: how would you describe your general sense of

well-being? Which is closest to the way you would describe yourself?

I feel healthy, alive and addicted to life	5
I feel pretty good most of the time and I enjoy my life	4
Sometimes I feel a bit low but generally I make the best of things	3
I wouldn't say I feel great most of the time	1

12 Health: how healthy are you, and do you take care of yourself?

I am fit and healthy and I enjoy maintaining a healthy lifestyle	4
I generally look after myself, but I like to enjoy the good things in life as well	3
I have some health problems, but I make the effort to do my best within that	2
Healthy or unhealthy, I don't pay attention to my health and consistently do things that I know are bad for me	0

13 Television: on average, how much time do you spend watching TV each week?

Less than four hours	4
Four to ten hours	3
Ten hours or more	1
I watch TV a lot, sometimes most of the time	0

14 Your sense of autonomy: how much do you feel in charge of your own life?

I feel I am in charge of my life, as much as anyone can be	5
I have a lot of autonomy in my life, though I still allow others to influence me more than I really want	3
I have some autonomy but it is restricted	2
I don't have much say at all in how my life goes, and there's not much I can do about this	0

15 Do people generally describe you as cheerful or joyful? Do you laugh a lot or make others laugh?

I am generally pretty cheerful and laugh a lot	4
I am cheerful most of the time and laugh sometimes	3

I am kind of average, quite cheerful, but I wouldn't say
I laugh that much　2
I can't say I feel cheerful or have much to laugh about　0

16　Do you blame or criticise yourself when things go wrong, you make mistakes, or you don't initially succeed at something?

No　4
Yes, some of the time　2
Yes, a lot of the time　1
Yes, all the time　0

17　Learning from life experience: would you say you learn a lot from your life experience and this changes the way you do things over time?

Yes, a great deal; I have changed a lot as a result of things I have learned　4
Yes, I learn from experience; some of it I can put into practice　3
I learn stuff but it doesn't usually change what I do in practice　2
I learn things, but it's other stuff that needs to change, not me　0

18　Self-image: would you say the image you have of yourself is similar to the one that others have of you? Or different?

As far as I know, the way other people see me is pretty consistent with the way I see myself　3
I feel there is a marked difference between who I really am inside and what other people see　0

19　On a normal day, when you don't have anything really difficult to face, how do you feel when you wake up in the morning?

I look forward to the day　4
I feel okay about the day　3
I don't feel too good about the day　0
I dread the day　0

20　Would other people say that you are an optimist or a pessimist?

An optimist. I see the good in most things, and I look forward to what the future may bring; people have commented on my sunny, or rose-tinted, view of life	4
An optimist, although I am also realistic when necessary	3
Neither one nor the other; I take life as it comes	1
There are a lot of serious problems and I don't see much to be optimistic about	0

21 **When making a decision, who do you consider?**

I do what is right for me, but I always consider other people's point of view, and how it will affect them	3
I consider other people more than I consider myself	1
I mainly consider myself	0

22 **Have you achieved any of your childhood ambitions or dreams?**

A great many of them	4
Some of them	3
None of them	1
I can't remember having any	0

23 **Do you have opportunities to help others in your work or daily life?**

Yes, I spend a lot of my time looking after or helping others	4
Yes, I spend some time looking after or helping others	3
I don't spend any time looking after or caring for others	0

24 **Do you feel valued and appreciated, both for what you do, and for who you are?**

Yes, a lot of the time	4
Yes, sometimes	3
I do sometimes feel valued, but I feel other people don't appreciate me enough	1
I very rarely feel appreciated or valued for what I put in	0

25 **Do you have spiritual beliefs, or an interest in spiritual matters that has been helpful to you?**

Yes	3
No, or don't know	0

Score
Write your happiness score here: _____

Over 70
You are an exceptionally happy person – you must know this already. Whatever you have is something that the rest of us would buy if you could bottle it – a sunny disposition, combined with a positive attitude, good self-confidence, firm beliefs in the things you strive for and believe in, and your share of good fortune. You have invested yourself wholeheartedly in your life, and you love the dividends that this has brought you. Without wanting to make you feel too smug, there are things people can learn from you about how you have succeeded in making your life feel rich, rewarding and fun.

50–70
You are an exceptionally happy person, and you are generally cheerful, constructive and make the most of whatever's going. You enjoy life and don't waste time on negativity or complaining. You are a positive influence.

35–50
You are generally a happy person and you like to make the most out of life.

Below 35
There are times when you don't feel particularly happy, and your score indicates that this may be the time to do something about this. Can you find a way to accept the things you can't change, and do something different with the things you can influence? It is possible you are on your own with this too much. How about selecting a friend to be a 'happiness buddy' – someone to share and enjoy with. Try selecting activities and relationships with the specific intention of using them to help build your happiness.

What is getting in the way of your potential happiness?

_____
_____
_____
_____

Keep a happiness journal

A research project that asked participants to keep a happiness journal showed that those who kept the journal reported feeling significantly happier and more positive than the control participants who didn't keep a diary. This is a simple way to focus on and expand your potential for happiness. In your journal, ask yourself questions such as:

- What does being happier and more blissful mean to me?
- What are all the possible positive outcomes of this week's events?
- Have I become more positive?
- Am I becoming more optimistic?
- Do I feel more confident and creative?
- Am I experiencing more positive coincidences?
- Am I listening to my intuition and inner feelings more?
- What am I doing to bring about positive change?
- How am I investing in a happier life?

Exploration and fun

Is there enough fun in your life? Funnily enough, we need fun in order to be healthy, both as children and as adults. Some people don't get enough opportunities for fun and adventure when they are children, and this can restrict their repertoire later in life. Fun doesn't have to involve much expense, but it might take some imagination, as staying home in front of the TV is definitely not that much fun. Do you allow enough space in your life for fun, adventure, exploration and exciting companionship? These questions are designed to raise your awareness of the fun dimension in your life, past and present.

1. As a child, what did you use to find fun?
2. What made you laugh?
3. What were your most exciting adventures?
4. What did you most love doing?
5. Who did you enjoy fun and excitement with?
6. What messages did you receive from adults about enjoying yourself?
7. As an adult, what do you find fun?
8. What are the main ways in which you have a good time? Is there enough variety?
9. How do you spend most of your spare time?
10. Who would be a good person to go on an adventure with?
11. If time and money were not a problem, what are some of the things you would really love to go and do?

Creativity

Creativity is a spontaneous expression of the self. Living itself, living your own authentic life, is a creative art. The novelist Joseph Conrad wrote in an introduction to one of his stories that 'the artist appeals to that part of our being ... which is a gift and not an acquisition – and therefore, more permanently enduring'. That part of us that is creative is an innate part of our being, and endures throughout our life. Creativity is not a commodity. All kinds of creative work can be done for their own sake. Whether or not they then have a financial value is not automatically relevant to their creative value.

How creative are you? Do you have the potential to be more creative? People differ widely in the amount of creativity they show in their daily life and in what kind of creative contributions they make to the world. For example, there is a difference in the type and amount of *obsession*, *passion* and *commitment* used by someone who writes music as a lifelong career, and someone who writes a song occasionally. Creativity research has been exploring what conditions foster creativity in individuals, and whether creativity can be deliberately developed and enhanced. In studies of creative people, certain types of personal profile are starting to emerge. It is also clear that creativity can be fostered by certain conditions. Surprisingly, many impressively creative people have survived far from perfect conditions, such as childhood deprivation, bereavement or neglect, and have used their painful experiences as a kind of driving force in their lives and work. The good news about this is that you do not have to feel discouraged by difficulties in life, for example time pressures, but you need to fight back for the right to your own form of personal creative expression. There is no need to wait until you have 'enough time' or 'the right space' – just do what you can do. If you have particular passions or obsessions, it's important to make time for them.

Creativity is a tool for life, not just for 'art', and it is really nothing to do with the 'tortured artist' archetype. Creative people demonstrate certain survival skills or life skills that help them think for themselves and find their own unique solutions. There is a connection between our creativity and our ability to deal with stress factors. People who think creatively can meet the challenges of self-doubt and low confidence, or problems and crises in life. They demonstrate an ability to come up with one-off custom-made solutions to situations that other people might find worrying or defeating. If they can't get a job they start a small business; if the small business takes a long time to get off the ground, they diversify. As the saying goes, when life brings them lemons, they make lemonade – and the lemonade is so delicious that everyone wants it and soon their problem is being able to find the right bottling plant. Creative people can see that although lemonade wasn't very desirable a few years ago when it became a mass-produced and tasteless commercial product, times have changed and people are wanting it again.

Creative people demonstrate traits such as a strong sense of self, self-discipline, flexibility, open-mindedness, hopefulness and optimism, and self-responsibility. They know that every cloud really does have a silver lining, and that eventually they will find it. Instead of feeling victimised when bad things happen, they set themselves a new learning opportunity. These are people who are hard to pigeon-hole, who reinvent themselves from time to time, and who can appear to others to be contradictory – for example, creative women can work independently and assertively in male-dominated careers without compromising their nurturing and empathic abilities. Whether or not you see yourself as a 'creative type', you can make use of a creative approach to life.

Cultivate the skill of asking yourself creative questions. Do this whenever a problem comes up. Do it whenever you get that vague sense of unease that things aren't entirely the way you want them to be. The skill in moving ahead lies in asking yourself the right questions. These are questions that encourage you to be inventive, imaginative, synergistic, playful, original, open-minded and curious. They are questions that get you off the old tram-lines of 'what everyone else thinks'.

Creative questioning

When you are asking yourself these questions, give yourself time and space to process them fully. Go into a relaxed state. Use your imagination. Contact how you really feel inside, and ignore the glib or superficial intellectual answers that may come up.

1. What is my special, unique learning opportunity in this situation?
2. Imagine yourself in the future. Look back on your situation five or ten or even twenty years from now. How does it look? With the benefit of hindsight, what would you do differently? Or the same?
3. How can I apply my core strengths to this situation?
4. How can I handle this so it will turn out well for everyone?
5. What is the possible long-term good of this situation?
6. What would happen if I did X? What would happen if I acted completely differently?
7. Am I maintaining a positive, optimistic outlook about the situation? If not, am I limiting my ability to problem-solve creatively with some negative expectations?

Apply your own creative questions:

Personal creativity

No one can dictate to you what is a creative way to live your life, do things or make things, or just be you. What is important is that you feel you can engage in authentic self-expression. Whether this is spending hours dreaming and daydreaming, creative home-making, journal writing, building a log cabin, building a collection of treasured objects, creating a new brand of designer accessories, creative science, or fostering creativity in others such as kids is entirely up to you. If anyone limits, questions or tries to control your creative time, you need to be fiercely protective. You don't need to explain to anyone else what you are doing, as it takes time to gather energy for a project and for a time it may look as if nothing is happening on the outside. People may think you are crazy if you spend all day designing embroidered gloves, but if they can't see the point, it may be because they have not developed their own creativity.

The creativity questionnaire

Section A
Circle **A**, **B**, **C** or **D** after each question (one only for each question).
A = a lot like me;   B = mostly like me;
C = not much like me;   D = not me at all.

1. Do you have a broad range of interests? — A B C D
2. Do you have a wide variety of hobbies? — A B C D
3. Do you have a strong sense of unique individual identity? — A B C D
4. Would you describe yourself as independent in your thinking? — A B C D
5. Would you describe yourself as playful? — A B C D
6. Would you describe yourself as imaginative? — A B C D
7. Are you open to a wide range of new experiences? — A B C D
8. Are you more unconventional than conventional? — A B C D
9. Have you produced a lot of work in your particular field of creative interest? — A B C D
10. Can you rise to a variety of different challenges? — A B C D
11. Do you have an individual or original approach to problem solving? — A B C D
12. Have you been able to use difficult situations and personal distress as a driving force for creative work? — A B C D
13. Are you strongly motivated to pursue creative challenges? — A B C D
14. Was there space allowed for you to develop your creative interests as a child? — A B C D
15. Have you or close family members suffered from psychiatric symptoms? — A B C D
16. Have you engaged in intense study and practice in your chosen creative areas? — A B C D
17. Are you good at generating new ideas in almost any situation? — A B C D

18 Do you enjoy making use of serendipity, i.e. chance encounters or discoveries? A B C D

19 Are you surrounded by people who love and respect you, and who would support and celebrate your creative achievements? A B C D

20 Even when you are really busy do you generally find time for some creative pursuits? A B C D

Section B

Again circle **A**, **B**, **C** or **D** after each question, but note that the order of the answers has been changed around, so that A = not me at all; B = not much like me; C = mostly like me; D = a lot like me.

1 Do you have a very firm or fixed belief system so that you nearly always know how to interpret information and events? A B C D

2 Are you highly self-critical? A B C D

3 Do you fear criticism of your work? A B C D

4 Are you afraid of what other people may think of you? A B C D

5 Do you suffer from being far too busy? A B C D

6 Do you suffer from having to deal with too many conflicting demands? A B C D

7 Was your time closely controlled when you were a child and teenager? A B C D

8 Do you have problems with pressure from family members if you want to focus on something? A B C D

9 Do you lack a space of your own where you can be alone to dream, think, read, play, write, and do the things that are important to you? A B C D

10 Do you believe that you are not creative? A B C D

Scores

Now add up the total number of each score:
A's _____ B's _____ C's _____ D's _____

The maximum possible number of each score is 30.

You have the highest number of A's

You are a true creative, and you probably already know this. You are likely to feel extremely uncomfortable, even unwell, if you do not have enough appropriate creative outlets. Your creative drive is central to your sense of self, and this makes you different from people who do not have this same degree of drive. You have at least one creative passion, and this is what you most love to do. The degree to which you are committed to a life of creativity is expressed in the score. Anything above 20 means you are devoted to your creative passions and obsessions and you have learned to make time for them, no matter what. You may well be capable of making a living from creative work if you so choose, and if your belief in yourself is also robust enough. If your score is below 20, it is possible you have had to fight for your right to be a creative, and this may not be over yet. Hopefully this questionnaire has refocused you on your creative identity, which needs to be a primary focus in your life. Make sure you receive enough high quality creative stimulation to avoid blocks or drying up.

You have the highest number of B's

You are a naturally creative person, and you bring this quality to a wide range of activities and situations. You bring along your unique creative contribution with you wherever you go, and you are good at solving problems and coming up with fresh solutions. You have a great sense of humour. You are also likely to have some serious, lifelong creative interests. Hopefully you have also created the opportunity to develop these, and you give them time and attention whenever possible. If you have not already done so, you could benefit from further training, study or practice in your field, and you would gain from the company of like-minded people with whom to discuss your work. Perhaps you need to develop more skills or confidence to move ahead to increase your A scores. Make sure you get the stimulation of enjoying high quality creative work by others in many different fields, whether it's opera or neuropsychology.

You have the highest number of C's

Inside you there is a creative person longing to come out – and you long for self-expression. It is possible you were overly restricted as a child, or that you have lacked opportunities to grow and develop this part of yourself. If you also have some A's and B's, it is really important to take this aspect of yourself much more seriously. Unexpressed creativity often creates a sense of frustration, feeling stuck, not knowing what to do next, or feeling bored. Start by making something easy. Just take one step each day and make sure you allow time for new activities. A good idea is starting a creative notebook or scrapbook – write down any ideas that come to mind, without censoring them. Writing in the morning just as you come out of sleep can be very helpful. It's best if you don't read what you have written for several months, then go back over it, hunting for themes and your hidden creative obsessions.

You have the highest number of D's
Creativity is not your primary language, and you can find creativity, and creative types, quite mystifying. However, if you have got this far, you know you want to learn to develop your creativity. Try talking to creative people about their work, or take a course in a subject that has always interested you. Follow the advice for C's, above, and also make sure you do everything you can to develop your confidence and self-esteem. Do you suffer from anxiety? Take a relaxation or meditation course, because your brain will be able to think more clearly if you are relaxed. Develop a flexible attitude to creative work, and try engaging in a wider range of activities in general, so that both the left and right sides of your brain are given a work-out. It is understood that creativity often involves a synthesis of both left and right brain activity. If you are only involved in left-brain activity in your daily work, this could be giving you tunnel vision. Reading novels and poetry, going to public lectures and visiting art galleries are a few ways to stimulate your creative centres because artists and innovators look at things differently and challenge our routine perceptions.

The 'miracle question'

This question is used in solution-focused counselling to motivate people to look beyond their current restrictions and limitations, and to evoke their creative imagination to help them to change.

Imagine you wake up tomorrow morning, and everything has changed. A miracle has happened. You feel peaceful, relaxed and happy. Worries that were troubling you have simply gone away.

Dreams that seemed far-off or even unlikely have been realised overnight. Nothing is missing in your life and you feel complete.

Spend time enjoying and exploring what this feels like inside. Make sure you capture all the details of how you feel, and what has changed.

Now have a good look at your miracle scenario. What does it say about you?

___

What are the elements of your miracle scenario that are already in place?

___

What are the elements that you have already been working towards and preparing for?

___

What remains for you to do in order to complete the scenario?

___

What are the further steps you need to take to complete the scenario as closely as possible to how your imagination sees it?

___

Give yourself a time frame to complete the different steps.

Creative problem-solving

Solving problems can be fun if we can get out of the way of the difficult and uncomfortable feelings that problems bring with them. It is often worry, fear and anxiety that prevent us having a fresh look at the problem-solving process. People who spend a lot of time doing crossword puzzles are not scared of them, but enjoy the mental exercise involved. Sometimes the solution is something original and comes from an entirely different way of thinking. Spend some time looking at a current problem. Use the questions to help you look at it differently and find a range of innovative solutions.

1. Define the problem. Clearly identify and describe the problem as you currently perceive it.

2. Gather facts about the problem. Research and study different aspects of the problem in general. For example, if your problem is that you feel lonely, then look into the causes of loneliness in your life. Immerse yourself in your studies about loneliness so that you really get to know and understand the subject. Look at how different people in different situations deal with this problem. You don't have to evaluate – just explore and acquire information. Talk to other people about loneliness and how they handle it. Try to get some personal distance from the problem: it's not just your problem, it's a wider human situation. Write a journal about your experiences and findings.

3. Redefine the problem. Is the definition of the problem 100% accurate? For example, is the problem not that 'I feel lonely' but that 'I don't have enough opportunities to meet people I find stimulating'. Be precise and accurate about the real origin of the problem.

4. Brainstorm new ideas on a big sheet of paper. Come up with all the solutions you can possibly think of. (It's even better if you can do this with a group of friends.) However ridiculous they are, don't censor your ideas or hold back, but write them down. Allow the ideas to keep coming. You are looking for quantity, not quality. Don't start analysing or criticising any of the ideas. Don't start thinking about how impractical or silly they are. This is playtime for ideas, and you will be surprised at how many different ones you can come up with if you let yourself. When you have finished, put the paper away for a

few days. Sleep on it. Forget about it and let the problem sort itself out for a few days. Be open to receive any insights that come to you.

5. Now start considering some real practical solutions. What are the feel-good bits you can pull off your sheet of paper? Put together ten viable solutions to your problem, solutions that some people would be willing to carry out, even if you are not quite sure about them.

Your ten solutions:

A _____

B _____

C _____

D _____

E _____

F _____

G _____

H _____
_____
_____

I _____
_____
_____

J _____
_____
_____

6   Run through your list of 'solutions'. Which ones feel right to you? Which ones would you be prepared to try out? Run through them and imagine yourself trying each of them out. Check how you feel internally as you do this. *What keeps you from feeling sound as you try out the solutions?* As you explore this, you may redefine the problem further. At this point in the process, the problem will look and feel different than it did when you started. Be open to new ways of looking at it.

Put into practice the solutions that seem the most friendly to you, and if these don't work you still have your list to come back to.

Well-being

Research in psychology was at one time restricted to psychological distress and illness, and our models of psychology were to some extent based on an understanding of pathology rather than on what helps or enables people to feel good and enjoy psychological and emotional well-being. This has changed, and now researchers in positive psychology are exploring the feel-good factors in life and how we can make the most of them to optimise our well-being.

Well-being can be defined as a state of all-round health and happiness. This includes social, physical, environmental and psychological dimensions, which all interact.

Criteria for well-being

Some researchers have come up with a neat definition of six measurable criteria for well-being. Consider how highly you score on each of these. Give yourself a score out of five for each one.

Self-acceptance
This is about having a positive attitude towards oneself, accepting how one is, and acknowledging all the different aspects of oneself and one's past experience.
Your score out of 5: _____

Positive relationships
This includes the ability to have warm, nurturing, open, intimate and trusting relationships, to be capable of deep empathy, to have concern about the welfare of others, and to feel deeply connected with others. While both men and women report that this dimension is central to their sense of well-being, it appears that women show greater strength in this area.
Your score out of 5: _____

Autonomy
A person with a high degree of autonomy runs their life according to their own values, is inner-directed, and can make their own decisions. He or she is able to withstand social pressures to conform or to think and behave in ways that do not suit them.
Your score out of 5: _____

Environmental mastery
This includes the ability to make the most of opportunities as well as to control one's everyday activities. It refers to someone who feels competent in managing their external world, and who can create or choose environments in which they can do well.
Your score out of 5: _____

A sense of purpose
Someone who has a sense of purpose in life has values and goals, they feel that there is meaning to their life, and that they have a sense of direction and reasons for living.
Your score out of 5: _____

Personal growth

A person who experiences personal growth is interested in life and learning. They understand that they are growing and developing, and they are open to new experiences throughout life. They see how their behaviour, skills, knowledge and attitudes all improve over time, and they develop increasing self-effectiveness and wisdom.

Your score out of 5: _____

Score

Your total well-being score out of 30: _____

If you score less well on one or two, try focusing your attention on those areas. Look at which of your values and goals you could use to support and increase this dimension of your well-being. If you work on it, you will find your score will increase over time. Come back to these questions after a few weeks or months.

chapter 6
relationships and communication

'There are few stronger predictors of happiness than a close, nurturing, equitable, intimate, lifelong companionship with one's best friend.'

– David Myers, happiness researcher

Across many nations and cultures, people who describe themselves as 'married' consistently report that they are considerably happier than non-married people. In addition, married people or people involved in a close romantic relationship or partnership have less depression, perhaps because a close relationship helps hold people together when times are bad. As we saw in the previous chapter, a healthy and happy marriage, or its equivalent, is a powerful contributor to happiness. On the other hand, relationships breaking up – as they often do – are a cause of great distress. We need relationships to make us happy, but they don't always last very long. When they break down we can feel that we have failed; separations are often angry, bitter and painful.

Are you happy in your relationship? What goes wrong? What makes relationships such hard work? Some hard work comes with the territory – but if you went to a couples therapist, there are specific features of your relationship the therapist would focus on, and specific processes she would engage in with you. This is because research has shown that certain relationship behaviours and attitudes, for example an attitude of *appreciation*, *acceptance* and *respect* towards a partner's individuality and foibles, are indicative of long-term satisfaction. Conversely, there are attitudes and behaviours, such as not listening to your partner, which clearly indicate low relationship quality and can predict relationship breakdown. There are hallmark positive and negative relationship behaviours. The good news is that relationship skills can be learned, and can be improved over time.

You can use this chapter to coach yourself in the fundamentals of maintaining good relationships. You can use it to diagnose where your relationship is now and where you want to go next.

If you are not in a current relationship you can use the questionnaires to evaluate what went wrong in the past and to determine your goals and values for a relationship in the future. Either way, these quizzes will help you understand that successful relationships are not as much a matter of luck or chance as people think. Relationships thrive or fail based on how people (a) perceive and (b) treat each other. Successful relationships are achieved when two equal partners continually demonstrate a high level of involvement, trust, commitment and emotional openness to each other, and are both prepared to take responsibility for nurturing and protecting the relationship. This takes continuing effort from both parties. Both people must give and take equally, although each will bring different strengths and skills.

Do you know a happy couple whose relationship you consider to be a success? Do you know a couple who seem to be continually in crisis with one another, or a couple who engage in constant arguments? Observe their couple behaviours. What works, and what doesn't? When she criticises him, what effect does it have on him? When he stonewalls her, what message is he giving her?

This section applies equally to all types of sexual and partnership relationship, whether heterosexual or gay. There is no assumption that the traditional marriage arrangement is the only type of 'normal' relationship.

If you are in a relationship, you can use these quizzes in various different ways. You can fill them in for yourself. You can fill them in for yourself and also write in what you think your partner's answers would be. If your partner agrees, you can both fill them in and compare your answers. Another thing you can do is guess each other's answers, and then see how accurate you were. You can then discuss your results and you will have a lot of material to work with.

All these processes will help you focus on and think about your relationship and move it on. It is possible they will illustrate and bring out the differences between you. When differences are revealed, conflict can arise. If this happens, establish some ground rules about how these conflicts are to be handled.

Couples exploration questionnaire

Answer this quiz both individually and as a couple. This will open up lots of areas for individual and mutual reflection, exploration and discussion. Don't try to answer all the questions at once – this is a really long questionnaire and the benefits are in the process of reflecting and coming to understand each other better, rather than in getting the answers down.

	Partner 1	Partner 2
Do you love each other?		
How would you describe your feelings towards your partner?		
How would you describe their feelings towards you?		
Describe your parents' relationship, as it was when you were growing up. What can you remember?		

	Partner 1	Partner 2
What did you learn about differences in roles between men and women?		
Remember and describe a typical scenario between your parents. For example, how did they handle conflicts or disagreements? Did they offer you a good role model for how to negotiate differences?		
What is the same and what is different about how you yourself handle conflicts and disagreements in your current relationship?		

	Partner 1	Partner 2
How did your parents negotiate closeness and distance?		
What messages and attitudes did your parents teach you about relationships from the way they ran their relationship?		
Can you see any similarities in the way you run your own relationships?		

	Partner 1	Partner 2
What do you find most fulfilling in your current relationship?		
What are the qualities you most appreciate and love about your partner?		
Do you both work actively to build and support the relationship? Do you do this equally?		

	Partner 1	Partner 2
Do you each support your partner's growth and development?		
What was the first major disillusion or disappointment in your relationship?		
How did you each deal with this at the time?		
How do you feel about this now?		

	Partner 1	Partner 2
Describe a typical scenario of the way you both currently handle problems, disagreements and difficulties in your relationship.		
How do you feel about this? Would you like it to be different?		
What do you find most challenging or difficult in your relationship?		

	Partner 1	Partner 2
Is there one thing you would like to change about your partner? If so, is there one thing that you would be willing to change in exchange?		
Do you feel safe being open, vulnerable, honest and disclosing sensitive feelings with your partner? Can they do this with you?		
In what ways are you both similar or the same?		

	Partner 1	Partner 2
In what ways are you different? How do you compromise on your differences?		
What are the separate skills, abilities and benefits each of you brings to the relationship?		
Do you feel there is a fair and equal exchange in your relationship?		

RELATIONSHIPS AND COMMUNICATION

	Partner 1	Partner 2
How easy is it for you to discuss sex and your sexual needs with your partner?		
How easy is it for you to discuss money and your financial position?		
What would you like your partner to help you with more?		

	Partner 1	Partner 2
Do you feel your partner gives you enough attention? What would you like more of?		
What are the things you most appreciate and enjoy about your relationship? Which aspects would you like to develop further?		
Do you have enough shared playtime as a couple?		

	Partner 1	Partner 2
Do you have shared commitments? How do these affect your relationship?		
Do you spend time doing things separately from your partner? How do you both feel about the other person doing things away from you?		
Are you able to maintain separate friends and interests?		

	Partner 1	Partner 2
Are you in agreement about core issues such as parenting skills or how you want things to be around shopping, housework, finances and meals?		
For you, what is the purpose of your relationship?		
What goals do you have for your relationship over the next year?		

RELATIONSHIPS AND COMMUNICATION

	Partner 1	Partner 2
What goals do you have for your relationship for the next five years? And beyond?		
What goals do you have for yourself over the next year and five years? How will these affect your relationship? How will your relationship impact on your individual goals?		

The relationship phases cycle

Each relationship is a journey. It passes through a natural series of phases and changes as it develops and matures. Once you know them, these phases are easily recognisable in other couples from the outside, but not so easy to understand when you are caught up in them. These developmental stages are comparable with the stages of growth and development that infants and young people go through to reach maturity. We are all involved in ongoing growth and development and these phases are never perfectly completed. Sometimes we also move backwards in order to complete something that we weren't able to finish before. However, each stage builds on the previous stage, and no phase can be skipped. Early childhood development can also affect your relationship, because issues that you had at each developmental stage as a child may be triggered when you reach the equivalent stage in your relationship.

If you know where you are in the relationship phases cycle, you can understand a lot of the difficulties you may be facing and what you can do about them. Each phase brings up a particular set of challenges and conflicts.

Each phase of the relationship journey has its own particular challenges that must be mastered before the couple can move on. The phases move from the euphoria of falling in love to the depth of real intimacy – if the developmental tasks of each phase are achieved successfully.

Each phase has a purpose. Each phase also has a time limit – eventually it needs to give way to the next phase. There is no set time that each phase needs to take, and sometimes they can take years to work through, but it is usually clear when a particular phase has passed its sell-by date. Things don't feel so good the way they were and you recognise that changes need to be made to keep things feeling good and healthy for both of you. Aspects of your relationship have to be renegotiated. However, you take with you to the next stage all the ground you have gained and the things you have learned.

When transitions from one phase to another start occurring, couples can feel confused, insecure, or can fall into conflict because they don't understand the changes that are happening to them. The transitions between phases are a time when most couples experience difficulties, and these are the times when many relationships break up. These transitions are never easy and straightforward for anybody. However, understanding the transitions as part of a healthy developmental sequence can be encouraging and helpful.

An additional complication is that an individual can arrive at the next phase of the relationship at a different time from their partner, rather than at the same time. Then the relationship consists of aspects of two phases. When this occurs, there are some particular difficulties to be negotiated, and there is often conflict, a sense of misunderstanding, betrayal or loss. For example the partner who has remained unchanged in the initial symbiotic stage may not understand, or may feel threatened by, what appears to be a sudden change in their partner who all of a sudden doesn't want to spend so much time alone with them, and wants to go out and attend to other commitments without them.

What phase is your relationship in? Are you and your partner both at the same phase, or are you at different phases? When you are in different phases, the conflicts need to be negotiated from a standpoint of recognising and appreciating each other's differences and individuality.

Choose one of the following five stages. It is possible that you and your partner could be in a different phase of development, so it is useful for you to consider these questions independently as well as together.

Which phase are you in?

Relationship phase 1: 'All about us'
This is the beginning phase of a relationship that everyone recognises as falling in love. You can't get enough of each other, and hold hands everywhere you go – if you even manage to get out of bed. There is passion, romance, and each person's needs are met to a high degree as they are receiving so much attention from the other person. Neither makes demands on the other person to change. Everything feels so exciting and pleasurable that neither person wants to risk the relationship by showing behaviour that might not be acceptable. You are adoring and adorable. When you are in this phase you emphasise your similarities and all the things you have in common. It is as if you have at last found someone who understands you perfectly and will meet your every need.

If after some months each person agrees the relationship is worth keeping, you then have a foundation on which to build. This symbiotic phase has a purpose. It enables you to make a firm bond or attachment. You spend a great deal of time gazing into each other's eyes and establishing tenderness and intimacy. This remains a source of strength and unity as you move on into the next phases. You can frequently return to this great feeling of belonging and closeness that underlies your relationship. Time spent in this phase is time well spent if your relationship is to be a long-term one. If it was never intended to be long term, when this phase ends conflict will start and it may be time to call it a day.

If you are in a relationship where this stage did not really happen or get completed, for example because of geographical distance or because life events got in the way, the attachment between you may never be as strong. If one or both partners are afraid of true intimacy, this phase may never get properly established, and the relationship will remain rocky throughout the future stages of its life.

If neither partner manages to achieve this stage fully, then this is a place where you can get stuck. You remain in the symbiotic stage in an unhealthy way. This can lead to problems such as an enmeshed or co-dependent relationship, where you try to remain merged, and you avoid conflict and expressing differences. A possible result of not wanting to move on from the symbiotic phase is a hostile-dependent relationship, where you get locked into continual cycles of conflict and pain. You can't bear to be apart and independent, and you can't bear to be together and co-operative.

Relationship phase 2: 'All about me and you'

This stage can happen just months after the first stage, or it can take a bit longer. It is often uncomfortable, because this is the time when you suddenly realise that you and your lover are different, and there are even some things about her or him that you don't like! This can be a real shock and you ask, 'What happened to the *us* feeling?' It can be a time of disappointment and disillusionment, and the depressing realisation that some of the promises made in Phase 1, such as 'I'll always take care of you', are a little unrealistic. Each person realises they have to take care of themselves as their partner has a separate life to them.

If the couple are to move on and stay a couple who have

negotiated this stage successfully, they have to start discussing things such as their individual expectations and needs, and to begin to work out a contract for the relationship.

Many relationships don't survive this transition, as this is when you may realise that the differences between you are just too big, and you can't imagine why you didn't notice them before. One or both of you may want to start spending less time together, for example seeing friends separately rather than doing everything together, or you may want privacy or time alone. The other partner can find this difficult, perhaps feeling excluded or rejected. If one or both of the partners is insecure or has low self-esteem, this can be a dangerous time.

The second phase also has a purpose. It's about each individual finding themselves again, and rediscovering the 'I' and 'me' that got put aside by 'us'. Each person has got to re-establish themselves as a separate and partly independent person. Without this, the relationship would stay stuck and neither person would be able to continue to mature and develop as an individual in their own right.

Relationship phase 3: 'All about me'

During this period, one or both people begin to engage more fully in separate activities. The individuals start to rediscover themselves as separate people. They go back to old friends or activities that their partner does not share, and may also develop exciting new interests or opportunities. Developing 'me' becomes more important for a while than developing 'us' or comparing 'you and me'.

This is when people start to think their partners are being incredibly self-preoccupied and selfish! The need for autonomy, self-expression and fulfilment seems to become much more important than the relationship, and the old sense of cosy security in each other may be temporarily lost. There can be a feeling that something precious has been lost, and that you are not in love any more. This can be a confusing time as there are so many conflicting interests. Each partner is fighting for independence and freedom, but also wants their partner to be there for them – on their terms and when they are ready for it. If one partner moves into this stage ahead of the other, it can be an incredible shock for the one left behind, who can feel abandoned. If both couples move into it around the same time, they may not see each other for dust. Attractions and affairs with other people may present a threat to the integrity of the relationship. These can create so much pain and anger that the processes involved may never be understood.

Again, this is a transition that some couples do not survive. Each person can be giving off the message 'I don't need you', and can feel incredibly trapped and restricted if their partner doesn't give them enough space. On the other hand, some people feel needy and clingy if their partner seems to abandon them for other pursuits and preoccupations and they feel they are no longer 'number one' in their lover's life.

This phase of development is similar to that of the two- to three-year-old child who wants to learn to do things independently and wants to do things herself without help. Then when something goes wrong, she expects Mum to be there instantly. This phase is also revisited by teenagers when they expect a high degree of autonomy and independence, but still expect their parents to pick up after them and pay all the bills. In these young people, the protestations of independence can be amusing or bemusing to adults. In the same way, some people going through this phase can give a strong message of 'Leave me alone and be here for me'.

Once this is understood and worked through, and the couple manage to establish their own blend of independence and togetherness, this phase enables each person to achieve more of their potential than they could have managed alone. They can move out into the world in a new way, confident that their partner is there for them behind the scenes. The couple learns the importance of trust and forgiveness or tolerance.

Relationship phase 4: 'Coming back to us'

After each partner has established a stronger sense of identity out there in the world and has started work in earnest on their own interests and development, it is safe to begin to start considering 'us' again. The couple starts to come back together again with more appreciation and understanding of each other's individual differences and needs. They spend more time together talking about the relationship and where they would like it to go.

There is a lot of work and attention given to the balance between 'us' and 'me'. The couple can fluctuate between periods of deep intimacy and connection, and periods of separation or independence when too much 'us' can still feel threatening to the individual's sense of self. The couple is caught between a fear of being engulfed in 'usness' or being too independent and alone. Couples may test out whether the other person is really there for them or not, or whether they will be allowed to have some life of their own without recriminations.

The issues of this period can cause conflict and unhappiness, as relationships can polarise. One partner may act out the need to be separate and will fear being engulfed by the other, while the other partner will act out the need for constant intimacy and will become clingy and demanding. Underlying issues about security and independence from childhood may also come to the fore.

Joe's mother was left by her husband, Joe's dad, when he was about four years old. She relied on Joe for emotional support, and when he became older she tried to subtly control and restrict his activities away from home so that he would usually stay home with her in the evenings. As a result, Joe feels allergic to women who seem to want to control his time, and he makes sure he is out every night. This behaviour creates the result that he dreads – a demanding, complaining woman waiting for him at home. He comes to see all women as whingeing and dependent, and decides he wants to live on his own so he will have 'enough space'.

If the issues of the fourth phase are successfully discussed and negotiated – which all takes time – the couple can eventually move on to greater contentment and depth.

Relationship phase 5: 'Interdependence'

After some years, the couple have developed some hallmark strengths: they know that they love each other, and they also feel engaged in their own individual lives. They are equally committed to both, and neither of these aspects is a threat. Each partner is an individual who finds security and satisfaction in their own life, and who also finds deep satisfaction in the relationship.

This is a stage of realistic compromise. Each person is willing to let go their hope for an ideal partner who will perfectly fulfil their every need. Each person is willing to put themselves out for the other, on the understanding that this is a mutual process. The couple put a lot of work into maintaining the relationship, through discussion and following through on their plans and agreements. They have become realistic and they don't expect the relationship to look after itself.

If one partner reaches this phase before the other, they may want increased intimacy and contact from a partner who is still at times trying to assert her or his independence. Patience may be needed.

Above all this is a stage of maturity, based on a sense of mutual respect and appreciation. Each person will encourage their partner to develop and grow, rather than try to make them meet their needs through control or manipulation. Openness and vulnerability increase. At this point each individual comes to understand how they must give to their partner even when it is not convenient, and they generally work towards the greater good of the relationship without feeling resentment about the compromises involved. They both recognise the profound value of the relationship. Although no relationship can ever be permanently taken for granted, the couple have achieved something solid and they feel ready to meet the future together.

Which phase are you in?
Can you identify the particular challenges you are facing in this phase of your relationship?

Rate your couple communication skills

Good communication is the essence of a good relationship. The likely success of a couple can be accurately predicted by observing their communications. This includes communications around greetings and partings, showing acceptance, listening, repairing conflicts, getting needs met, handling differences and disagreements, showing understanding and empathy, and managing everyday life. If the couple uses good interpersonal skills with each other, each person will feel respected, valued, understood, and that their individual needs are taken into consideration.

This quiz will help you assess and think about how good you are at communicating as a couple. It is a good predictor of how well your relationship will do in the long term – and which aspects of communication you can work on that will have a beneficial effect.

Think about how you are most likely to respond in the following situations as a couple.

1 **You both get together after long, tiring and stressful days. How do you handle the first part of the evening together?**

A One partner is preoccupied and doesn't pay much attention to the other.
B One or both of you gets into a negative mood.
C One of you tries to look after the other, but it doesn't feel equal.
D You sit down together and spend time reconnecting before you do anything else.

2 **When you have a conflict or disagreement about something major are you most likely to:**

A Misunderstand what the conflict is really about, or not accept the other person's version of it?
B Allow negative or critical conversations and arguments to occur?
C Both go in opposite directions and avoid the issue?
D Talk it through until you reach a compromise you can both live with?

3   You both desperately need a holiday. One of you wants a beach holiday to chill out, and the other hates beaches and wants an active trip. Is the most likely outcome that:

A   You go on the holiday that the most persuasive and dominant partner wants, and the other person feels uncomfortable but makes the best of it?
B   You go on the holiday the most persuasive partner wants, but the other never lets them forget it?
C   You go on separate holidays?
D   You find a holiday where you can both spend time doing things individually, as well as time together?

4   When you live together, how do you handle grocery shopping?

A   You go shopping together; sometimes it's a bit tense but you make the most of it.
B   You each buy stuff on an individual basis as and when, and there is some dispute about your choices.
C   One of you nearly always takes all the responsibility for this.
D   You discuss how it will be done, and either take it in turns, or find other ways to share the work, time and expense.

5   You have different opinions about a sensitive subject, and you definitely disagree with each other's views. Are you most likely to:

A   Avoid your differences and appear to agree?
B   Get critical and unhappy with each other?
C   Decide one of you is superior and has the right opinion?
D   Each listen carefully and accept the other's opinion, although you may still disagree?

6   Your partner is drunk and behaving in an embarrassing way at a party. Are you most likely to:

A   Try to pretend it isn't happening?
B   Get angry and critical?

C Feel it's not your responsibility and go home without them?
D Get them home safely, and find an opportunity to discuss what happened and how you felt about it the next day?

7 Your partner is busy and stressed, and is making a lot of demands on your time and resources. You are also pretty busy yourself. Are you most likely to:

A Drop everything to help them out, and do everything you can?
B Help them out, but then feel exhausted and exploited?
C Give them some good advice about how to manage their time better?
D Offer to help out as much as you can, because you know they will do things for you when you need it?

8 You have got definite ideas about what you want to do over the weekend. Your partner also has definite ideas about what he or she wants to do, and this involves your full participation. What is the most likely outcome?

A You both assume that you will be spending the weekend together.
B One of you is angry with the other for not fitting in or for spoiling your plans.
C One of you does exactly what they want, and if the other doesn't fit in – well, tough.
D You talk it through before the weekend arrives, and you settle on a compromise you can both live with.

Scores

Mostly A's
Generally you feel you have a close relationship. At times you can feel very close and that you have a lot in common. However, this doesn't in fact facilitate good communication all the time. You may be denying or avoiding the differences between you. You may not realise that you see things through two entirely different telescopes. You may assume that you know who your partner is and what they are feeling and thinking, but in fact they can still surprise

you. It would be helpful to listen more carefully to each other, and not make too many assumptions. You could also develop more open discussion and negotiation skills, and be more accepting of the ways in which their personality and needs are different from yours.

Mostly B's
While you have the basis of a good partnership, there is a lot of negative communication in your relationship, and this could reduce the value and longevity of the relationship for both of you. There is a tendency to withdraw, sulk or punish, or for one of you to feel justified in behaving badly. You allow negative conversations to occur, and this damages the trust and safety between you. It would be helpful to cultivate a more friendly and accepting climate, and to avoid expressing criticism and blame.

Mostly C's
There is a sense in which this partnership may not be a fully equal one. Is one of you putting in more sincere effort than the other? Is one of you very possessive? Does one of you express more care and concern than the other? Does one of you feel taken for granted? Do you gloss over problems so that you can't really move forward? What are the ways in which this relationship could become more of a friendship between equals? It might be a good time to put your cards on the table and decide if you are ready, willing and able to really give each other what you need.

Mostly D's
You demonstrate positive social behaviour between you. You are able to repair negative conversations, soothe tense situations, and open up discussions of sensitive issues in a friendly, open and accepting style. You listen to each other carefully and respectfully. You realise, and accept, that maintaining this relationship requires a lot of work, and you are equal partners and good friends in this. You have both found each other to be reliable and trustworthy partners and companions. You can work out compromises that meet both of your needs, and you are respectful and encouraging of your partner's growth and development as a separate person as well as being your partner. You give each other lots of rewards, contact and appreciation, and this makes being in the relationship a pleasurable experience for much of the time.

RELATIONSHIPS AND COMMUNICATION

Expectations

What do you expect of your partner? And what does he or she expect of you?

Getting both of your expectations clear and explicit helps to create a positive and constructive tone in your relationship. Expectations need to be balanced. There is no balance if one person is expected to do all the housework and the other person expects to sit there and be waited on – unless these expectations have been clearly agreed in advance and both parties have agreed that it is fair and desirable. This is an obvious example, but expectations can be more subtle than this, and they become difficult to erode as they can become part of the very fabric of the relationship.

When Amanda and Dan first got together, he soon found out that she was an excellent cook. On one of their first dates she suggested that he come round to her apartment and she would cook for him. She made it her job to create a highly seductive dinner scenario. Not only were there candles, soft lights, flowers, romantic music, incense and new bedlinen – she also cooked a knockout dinner. Of course, she had found out in advance about some of his favourite foods and food combinations, and she spent most of the day preparing for the evening.

When Dan arrived he had a fabulous time, and happily agreed to her seduction routine. He commented several times on how delicious the food was, asked how she had known that bouillabaisse was one of his most favourite foods – and told her the one she had made tasted even better than a fabulous one he had once had in Provence. Amanda saw that he enjoyed and appreciated good food, and so she continued to cook for him, asking him round to eat several nights a week. He was not able to return the favour, as he was still living with his wife while the arrangements for their divorce were being sorted out, and also he was short of money because his wife had taken him to the cleaners. When Amanda was out or unable to cook for any reason, he would go out to eat, and meet her afterwards. Then Amanda would fix herself a sandwich or some soup when she got in.

Because he didn't have anywhere to live once the divorce was finalised, it seemed sensible to Amanda that he should move in with her for the time being. As soon as she offered, he accepted, and within six months of their getting together he moved in. He offered to make a contribution to household expenses but she said she was happy for him to be her guest for the time being. For a while everything continued as before and they were happy. Dan would leave early for work, and Amanda would clear up the dinner from the night before and clean the apartment before she went to work a few hours later. She worked part-time because she was also building up a small business of her own from home. She found that when Dan moved in she was less able to concentrate on this, as most of her energy went on being with him.

As they settled into a routine over the next eighteen months, Amanda would sometimes encourage Dan to help out in the kitchen, but he explained that he was nervous about cooking and not very good at it. He was afraid he would never be able to live up to her standards. In fact he did make a few things, and he did seem to be useless in the kitchen – he would turn the oven up far too high and burn things, partly because he was expecting her to take things out of the oven at the right time.

Amanda only gradually realised that Dan expected her to cook for him every day, with minimal contribution from himself. He would give her some money for housekeeping from time to time, but he often seemed to forget, and it seemed to her he didn't have a realistic view of how much things cost. He seemed to assume that because she was 'buying it for herself anyway' and that she would have to pay the utilities bills anyway, there was no need for him to contribute much.

When she eventually challenged him about his expectation that she should do all the cooking he was quite offended, and didn't really want to discuss it. He implied that he didn't really want to be bothered with all that sort of thing, and that he had more serious and important worries on his mind, such as his divorce and his stressful move to a new law practice as a partner. Then he changed the subject to talk about how attractive she was and how much he fancied her.

Amanda realised too late how dumb she had been and that being in love with Dan and wanting to do everything possible to please him had prevented her from thinking straight. She had contributed to Dan's expectations that she would behave exactly like his mother, and do everything for him in the domestic department. Dan and Amanda had never spent any time discussing their mutual expectations of a partner in a relationship, and the situation had crept up on them both. Dan's expectations – which he had never spent much time examining – were that women did the trivial domestic stuff and men did the hard graft out in the world. He expected her to act in a supportive role to him. And because Amanda had led him on with her culinary seductions, he expected food of an equivalent quality to be on the table every night. Some of Amanda's expectations meshed with Dan's very well. She expected that she would be supportive and be a creative homemaker, and that she would be there for Dan whenever he needed her. But she also expected that he would make some kind of fair and equal contribution in some way, and while she patiently waited for this, it never seemed to come. She also expected support at times when she herself was working hard, or having some problems with her business. But she found that when she was tired, stressed or busy Dan would be particularly demanding. If she didn't manage to make dinner by the time he wanted it, he would go out to eat alone, and he wouldn't invite her along.

By the time she realised all this, Amanda felt despondent, and Dan didn't seem at all interested in discussing this. After some months of stressing about what to do, she asked him to leave. He seemed very hurt but said little, though he sent her a number of lavish floral gifts with romantic notes to 'my little bunny'. Amanda didn't feel brave enough to challenge him to discuss the issues that would have to be resolved if they were to move forward as a couple, and the relationship fizzled out. Dan found someone else almost immediately, while Amanda resolved to live alone for a while until she could sort out in her mind why her relationships seemed to be one big mistake after another.

If Amanda and Dan had clarified their expectations early on in their relationship, it might never have got off the ground. Who could admit to expecting a combination of mother, seductress and doormat as a partner? It was easier to fudge the issues involved. It would be easy to be critical of Dan, but in fact he was just operating along the lines of his conditioning – he wanted a quiet life, and Amanda had never seriously disrupted his view that she was a helpful little bunny who had come along just at the right time. Establishing and clarifying expectations as you go can make a lot of difference to the type of relationship you end up with.

> ### What are your expectations of a relationship?
> What are the bottom line qualities you must have from a partner?
> What are the qualities you would like from an ideal partner?
> What expectations do you feel you have of your partner?
> What expectations does she or he have of you?
> What expectations on either side do you feel uncomfortable with or are not fully met?
> Are your expectations of each other fair, realistic and equal? Is there a sense of balance in your relationship?

Making a contract

A contract is an agreement that two (or more) people decide on together, and then agree to keep to. It can be a great help to establish your own relationship contract, which is not something fixed in concrete and which needs to be reviewed on a regular basis. This is a good way of maintaining your relationship health, and helps you keep track of your expectations of each other and how things are turning out. It is not a legal contract, but an agreement that is explicitly discussed so that both parties know exactly what is expected of them, and what they can expect in return.

Positive and negative couple behaviours

Successful couple behaviours

Successful couples are engaged in almost continuous monitoring of their relationship, and take care to behave in a way that considers each person's needs equally. Successful couples can be taught how to become even more successful, and can learn to overcome problems in communication if they can identify and understand them. Certain behaviours convey to the other person that you care about them, you are sensitive to their needs, and you will respond to them when they need you to. This checklist includes a number of behaviours which, when combined, can help develop a healthy and happy relationship. It does not have to mean you are insincere if you learn and practise these behaviours, but in fact can demonstrate to your partner that you are making an effort to improve things.

Rate yourself and your partner

Positive couple behaviour

Tick each of the following that applies in your relationship.

		Partner 1	Partner 2
1	When your partner needs to raise a difficult topic, he/she does so kindly and gently, and chooses an appropriate time to bring it up.	☐	☐
2	Your partner treats you as an equal.	☐	☐
3	Your partner respects you.	☐	☐
4	He or she shows genuine care and concern for your welfare.	☐	☐
5	He or she does things for you happily and voluntarily.	☐	☐
6	Your partner considers your needs as much as his or her own.	☐	☐
7	Your partner encourages you to grow and develop.	☐	☐
8	Your partner satisfies you sexually.	☐	☐
9	He or she challenges you kindly and appropriately when necessary.	☐	☐
10	Your partner understands you.	☐	☐
11	Your partner is good at listening to you.	☐	☐
12	He or she accepts you for who you are.	☐	☐
13	Your partner is there when you need him or her.	☐	☐
14	He or she increases your self-esteem.	☐	☐
15	Your partner actively demonstrates love and appreciation for you.	☐	☐
16	Your partner frequently engages in affectionate physical contact, not just sexual.	☐	☐
17	Your partner has time for you.	☐	☐
18	Your partner is able to let go of past problems, disagreements and mistakes and move on.	☐	☐

19. He or she always seems to maintain a positive view of who you are. ☐ ☐

20. Your partner is sincere and honest in dealing with you. ☐ ☐

21. Your partner is always interested to learn more about you. ☐ ☐

22. You and your partner have discussed your past with each other in some depth. ☐ ☐

23. You feel your partner knows and understands some of your goals and dreams and supports them. ☐ ☐

24. Your partner accepts your influence in his or her life, and adapts his or her plans to suit you. ☐ ☐

How many successful couple behaviours did you tick? Partner 1 _____

Partner 2 _____

Negative couple behaviour

How many of these do you engage in? And your partner? This checklist reads like a manual for how to have a terrible relationship! These are all the things not to do. Each one of these behaviours signals trouble in a relationship if it is allowed to continue. If you find yourself engaged in any of these behaviours *on a regular basis*, it's time to stop and think.

Partner 1 Partner 2

1. Starting up an argument in an aggressive or critical manner. ☐ ☐

2. Frequent criticism. ☐ ☐

3. Nagging. ☐ ☐

4. Complaining. ☐ ☐

5. Not treating your partner as an equal, either regarding them as more or less equal than you. ☐ ☐

6. Not responding to reasonable requests. ☐ ☐

7 Giving in too quickly to unreasonable demands. ☐ ☐
8 Agreeing to accept unacceptable behaviour from your partner. ☐ ☐
9 Blaming your partner for the way you feel. ☐ ☐
10 Being reactive and defensive when your partner tactfully challenges or criticises you. ☐ ☐
11 Not listening. ☐ ☐
12 Not allowing them to influence you or adapting your plans to suit them. ☐ ☐
13 Stonewalling. ☐ ☐
14 Using body language that conveys indifference or lack of interest. ☐ ☐
15 Sulking or not speaking as a form of punishment. ☐ ☐
16 Frequent withdrawal. ☐ ☐
17 Acting out of jealousy. ☐ ☐
18 Being bossy. ☐ ☐
19 Being controlling. ☐ ☐
20 Being demanding that your needs are met, even if your partner is busy or unwell. ☐ ☐
21 Doing less than half the work. ☐ ☐
22 Refusing to talk about certain topics. ☐ ☐
23 Doing things that break your agreed contract as a couple. ☐ ☐
24 Refusing to accept responsibility. ☐ ☐
25 Being unappreciative or not noticing things. ☐ ☐
26 Holding grudges. ☐ ☐
27 Undermining your confidence and success. ☐ ☐
28 An expectation that you will take care of their needs – but not vice versa. ☐ ☐

29 Constant disagreements or arguments about day-to-day issues. ☐ ☐

30 Speaking badly about your partner to others. ☐ ☐

How many negative couple behaviours do you regularly engage in? Partner 1 _____

Partner 2 _____

What would you like to change?

RELATIONSHIPS AND COMMUNICATION

Healthy protest

The capacity to protest when you are not happy about something is healthy. We all need appropriate anger and assertiveness to make sure that our needs are properly met and we are not walked over or treated badly. These questions will help raise your awareness of the issues involved in healthy assertiveness.

As a child, could you say what you wanted, and be listened to?

Were you able to say 'No' to things you didn't want?

If you were upset or angry, how did you express it? Did someone take you seriously?

When you feel angry now, how do you usually handle it?

If your partner does something that really upsets you, how do you deal with it? (For example, do you express direct anger, do you withdraw and go quiet, do you sulk, punish them by making them feel as bad as you, go passive?)

Are you able to ask for what you want from your partner and other people close to you?

Do you ever feel taken for granted or exploited by your partner or other people close to you?

Do you ever feel your aggression gets out of control? Or that your anger is expressed in a very indirect and passive way?

These questions and answers will indicate to you some of what you learned as a child, and have put into practice since, about the rules surrounding your right to protest appropriately, ask for what you want, say no, and set limits on other people's behaviour towards you.

Managing conflict

Conflict occurs in all relationships, and just because there is conflict or you experience negative feelings towards your partner from time to time, it doesn't mean there is anything wrong. A successful and rewarding relationship is not one with a complete absence of negativity and differences, but one where the negativity and opposing views are honestly and kindly negotiated and worked with.

Conflict occurs for many reasons, all based on having a different point of view: personality differences, attachment styles and personal history, being at different stages in your development, transference (see chapter 4), misunderstandings in communication, and people wanting different things or having agendas of their own that make them want to drive a situation forward to meet their own needs. Sometimes your partner just does not realise he has done something to annoy or hurt you, because he has been completely preoccupied with something else.

A relationship where conflict cannot be expressed is not usually a healthy one. However, conflicts that are handled aggressively and unskilfully are the cause of endless heartache.

What is a fair fight? If your relationship is to remain healthy and move on it helps to agree to some shared guidelines. For example, some people grew up in families that were noisy and expressive, and using raised voices is part of their everyday life. Other people who grew up in quieter households, where raising one's voice was rare except to express extreme anger or frustration, can find being yelled at by their partner for forgetting to buy the onions completely unacceptable.

Acceptable and unacceptable behaviours

Consider these behaviours which may emerge in a conflict situation, and decide which of them are acceptable to you and which are not. If you and your partner disagree, then you need to reach a working compromise you can both keep to. Using any of these strategies usually reduces the chance of successful conflict resolution.

1. Shouting or raising your voice.
2. Swearing or using strong language.
3. Using physical aggression.
4. Bringing up the past or other things that are not directly related to the topic you are dealing with.
5. Starting an argument by criticising the person, or using criticism to bully the other person to change.
6. Withdrawing or refusing to engage, changing the subject, or ignoring what is said.
7. Not listening when the other person raises an important topic.
8. Raising the subject in a confrontational or aggressive tone of voice.
9. Blaming the other person for your own bad feelings.
10. Any other behaviour that you are not comfortable with.

During a fight or disagreement, which of the above are acceptable for you to engage in?

_____

_____

_____

_____

Which ones do you feel it is acceptable for your partner to engage in?

_____

_____

_____

Which ones are acceptable to your partner?

Which ones are not acceptable to your partner?

What agreements about behaviour do you need to make in order to feel confident your disagreements will be fair?

Skilful conflict management

Generally a conflict that is managed skilfully, using an effective communication style, is much more likely to reach an acceptable resolution – or at least the people concerned may agree to accept their differences. People can usually accept a level of disagreement, but not disrespect, blame or humiliation. A skilful approach to resolving a conflict includes these eight conflict management techniques:

- Choose and mutually agree on an appropriate time and place in which to have the discussion, not when either party is tired, stressed or preoccupied.
- Give yourself a mutually agreed time limit – don't continue arguing for hours.
- Think carefully about what you want to say before saying it; for example, do not take the opportunity to vent your worst and most negative feelings such as hostility and resentment. A successful argument is not a free expression of negativity, but an adult form of negotiation.
- Take it in turn to listen carefully to each party's point of view.
- Each person then paraphrases their understanding of what the other is trying to get across, as far as possible using the other person's language, and not adding in any angry distortions; for example, 'It seems you're saying that you feel you can't cope without me being here more and you need me to help more with the children,' is a better paraphrase than, 'You're always moaning that I'm not here. I thought you knew how busy I am.'
- Each person has space to express what is making them unhappy and what they want to change. This is expressed in respectful, non-blaming language; for example, 'When you slam the door I feel rejected and shut out,' not 'Why do you always have to slam the door, can't you shut it properly?'
- Any things you want the other person to change must be expressed as a positive request, such as, 'I would love it if you could bring me some tea in the morning before you leave; it would really make a difference to me,' rather than, 'You don't care about me any more, you never make me tea in the morning.'
- Try to reach a working compromise that is acceptable to both parties before you finish, even if the ideal solution will have to

wait. Agree on what both parties will do to improve the situation. Agree a future time to discuss how things are going.

Which of these eight techniques are you best at? Worst at?

Forgiveness and reconciliation

Sometimes letting go – or forgiving – what someone has done is the only way to free yourself and move on. Although it's probably not a good idea to forget hurtful things done to us, we can open ourselves up to a better future, rather than allow what happened to make us permanently miserable or permanently scar the relationship. While getting back at the person in some way can make you feel better temporarily, forgiveness seems to have better health benefits for the victim. Forgiving people have less anxiety and depression, show less hostile behaviour and are generally healthier. The ability to forgive may be related to the degree of satisfaction and closeness felt in the relationship – i.e., it is easier to forgive when you understand where the person was coming from when they did the thing that upset you. Interestingly, a low level of self-forgiveness is also associated with low self-esteem, anger and anxiety.

The forgiveness process can be seen in three stages:

1 **Can you acknowledge and discuss what has happened?** This means not denying or avoiding what has happened, and acknowledging that you feel the other person is to blame – otherwise there would be nothing to forgive.

2 **Can you detach yourself?** For example, can you feel empathy and understanding for what the person was feeling at the time and try to understand their motivations? If you feel anger, use this as a source of fuel to bring about positive change, if possible.

3 **Can you discuss it openly and honestly?** In order for forgiveness to be possible, the other person must be able to acknowledge the full extent of what they did to you, and to understand exactly how it made you feel. (Sometimes people will deny or minimise the importance of what has happened.) If they can't see the situation from your point of view, you won't be able to fully forgive them.

Personality differences

These are responsible for many conflicts, because we tend to assume people are the same as us and think exactly as we do – or that if they are different to us, then they are wrong. We sometimes fail to realise that other people may be wired completely differently to us, and that therefore we cannot automatically understand where they are coming from.

The most basic and profound personality difference is between extroversion and introversion. Even though this is now widely recognised and understood, this difference still causes many misunderstandings between couples. This is because these two fundamental types see and relate to the world in different ways. If you are an introvert it is hard to see things from an extrovert's point of view, and vice versa. Neither is better than the other, they are just different. Extroversion and introversion can be seen as different ends of a pole, and we are all somewhere between the two; most people have some qualities from both of these characteristics, but have a marked preference for one or the other. It is understood that to be either an introvert or an extrovert is part of the natural temperament that you are born with, so this is something you cannot fundamentally change. However, life experiences or situations may force us to take on characteristics and qualities from the other end of the pole. If you are an introvert, it doesn't mean you can't use extrovert skills when you are socialising. However, being an outgoing party animal will never come as easily and naturally to you as it does to a truly gregarious extrovert, and perhaps you would secretly prefer to spend the evening in the company of a good book, or with just one or two other people.

Are you an extrovert or an introvert?

Circle **A** or **B** for each question, then add up your score at the end.

1. If someone invites you to a large party, do you:

    A   Feel under pressure to attend?

    B   Feel energised and excited, and really look forward to it?

2. What does your circle of friends look like?

    A   You have a small group of loyal friends who you know well, and who you love to spend quality time with.

    B   You have a wide circle of many different types of friends, colleagues and acquaintances, all of whom you regard as friends.

3. Do you:

    A   Feel low and exhausted if you spend too much time with other people?

    B   Feel low and exhausted if you spend too much time alone or with just a few people?

4. Do you:

    A   Really enjoy your own company and feel you benefit from time alone?

    B   Find you can put up with your own company for a while?

5. If you had a weekend alone at home, would you:

    A   Feel content to stay home?

    B   Feel the need to get out, meet people or find entertainment?

6. Do you:

    A   Feel tired if you have to spend the day working intensively with other people?

    B   Feel energised by lots of contacts with people at work?

7 When you first come home from work, do you:

   A Like to do something quiet, peaceful and relaxing?
   B Find someone to talk to, or switch on the TV or radio?

8 Do you tend to:

   A Get intensely interested and involved in your favourite subjects or activities, and sometimes lose track of time?
   B Have a wide range of interests, but can easily move from one to another?

9 Do you:

   A Find it hard to concentrate in a noisy environment or when you are interrupted?
   B Enjoy having lots of activity around you, and quite enjoy being interrupted?

10 Would you say it is:

   A Quite difficult for people to get to know you quickly, and that people only appreciate and understand your depths after they have known you for some time?
   B Quite easy for people to get to know you?

Scores

Number of A's _____ (introversion)

Number of B's _____ (extroversion)

Compare your score with your partner's, and discuss this.

Communication and lifestyle preferences

These questions will have illustrated some of the differences in lifestyle preferences between extroverts and introverts. While each can accommodate the other, it is exhausting to live all of the time outside your natural preferences. If you are an introvert and work with people all day, you need a bit of time to yourself when you get home, or perhaps a one-to-one conversation where you have the opportunity to converse about something in-depth. If you are an extrovert and don't get enough contact during the day, you will be eager for company, fun and stimulus as soon as you get in.

Introverts gain their energy and inspiration from their inner world, while extroverts gain energy and inspiration from their outer world, so there are completely different requirements for external stimulation. In addition, introverts like time to think things over, they tend to think about things deeply, and then present you with the end result of their thinking process, which you can be sure has been carefully considered and mulled over for some time. On the other hand, an extrovert will think out loud in order to find out what they think about something, but this will probably not be their final word on the subject. Thus an introvert might think that an extrovert's off-the-cuff comments carry more weight than they really do, while the extrovert may not realise that the introvert has just uttered an incredibly important statement that may have taken them weeks of thought. Introverts can be sure that they have told you something – but in fact they have only thought it, and have not remembered to open their mouth and share it with you. Extroverts can tell you something so many times that you cease paying attention.

These differences in communication styles and lifestyle preferences are not just superficial, but indicate two fundamentally different approaches to thinking and to perceiving reality. Understanding, accepting and valuing each other's differences can make any relationship much stronger. Often introverts and extroverts are attracted to each other, as their differences, once understood, are complementary, and give the relationship greater strength. A relationship that possesses both qualities will be more balanced.

Security and attachment

Attachment is now understood to be a key feature of adult emotional life. From the beginning of life onwards, our physical and psychological health and security are based on our connections with other people. Self-esteem and emotional security are inextricably linked. In early childhood, this security is dependent on physical closeness; as adults, we need emotional proximity and nurturing, empathy and understanding. There is a great deal of evidence that secure attachment in childhood leads to healthy emotional and psychological behaviour in adults and less problematic relationships. Securely attached adults have a greater capacity for companionable relatedness.

John Bowlby was a British psychological researcher in the 1950s and 60s who pioneered the study of attachment, separation and loss. He found that children separated from their mothers (or primary carers) for too long started to show a range of psychological symptoms, which he described as attachment disorders. He found that as children we feel good about ourselves and our world if we have trustworthy adults we can turn to. Research by Bowlby's many followers eventually led to current practices in childcare, such as making it possible for parents to stay with children when they have to be in hospital. Before this, children's untold pain and suffering on having to be separated from their parents for various reasons – such as illness, family circumstances, 'resettling', or relocation due to war – were not fully understood. Many people have grown up without a secure base, and can attest to how this has always made them unhappy, insecure, and unable to maintain satisfying relationships.

Children who have experienced a secure feeling of attachment are well equipped to enjoy stable and secure relationships as adults. People who have less emotional confidence in others find it more difficult to relate. It is almost as if they are expecting something to go wrong, and they cannot fully relax in a relationship because they are always slightly anxious that they may be in for further abandonment, lack of safety, loss or even hostility.

Everyone demonstrates their own attachment style, which is a fusion of their experience as a child, their family attachment patterns, and their personality and preferences. There are four different styles of attachment: secure, anxious, avoidant and ambivalent. None of these are fixed, and most people show different combinations of these attributes at different times. If at least one of the partners in a couple shows a secure attachment style, the relationship has the potential to be more stable than that between two people who both exhibit features of anxious or avoidant attachment. People can develop much more self-confidence as adults if they find themselves in a relationship that offers them a sense of security. However, insecure people tend to repeat the past: they choose people who 'fit' into their past models, and where patterns of anxiety, hostility and fear of abandonment or entrapment can get acted out. This way they get some attention and feel alive.

Relationships go well when there is an underlying sense of security and stability. This is not to say that they have to become predictable and boring, but that at the end of the day you can usually count on your partner to be there for you. You are fairly confident that they are not going to run off with the cocktail pianist! Individuals who are secure in themselves are good at creating secure relationships. They do not create anxiety and hostility or make others feel insecure. They are also more likely to enable their children to feel secure as they do not resent their dependence.

What is your attachment style?

Which is *most* like you? (You may find it helpful to think back over previous relationships, as well as your current one, to see patterns that may become more recognisable over time.) There are just three sections to this; in each case, select which of the four 'answers' describes you best. These represent four attachment styles, which are described at the end.

A
How much do you need to feel close to your partner all the time, and how much do you need to maintain some distance?

1. You enjoy feeling close and connected with your partner. You can depend on them, and allow them to depend on you.
2. You enjoy feeling close and connected, but sometimes you worry whether the relationship will last.
3. You enjoy sex and closeness at times, but you prefer to maintain your independence, and to stay in control of how you feel.
4. You enjoy feeling close and connected, but sometimes this makes you feel trapped or claustrophobic. Sometimes you are not sure how you feel about being dependent on your partner, or having them rely on you too much.

B
When your partner goes away or is absent for a long period, which is closest to the way you feel?

1. You miss your partner, but you stay in close contact while they are away, and you look forward to them coming home. You use the time for other things such as seeing friends or getting work done.
2. You miss your partner, and this unsettles you for a while. You find it difficult to get on with life and you think about them a lot.
3. You hardly miss your partner, you make yourself so busy with other things; perhaps you see other people while they are away.
4. You miss your partner a great deal to begin with, but when

they come back you have got used to having your own independent life, and it is difficult to get used to them being around again. In fact, you are not 100% happy about seeing them again.

C

You are waiting for your partner to arrive home, and she or he arrives several hours later than you expected. For some reason they are unable to call you to explain. When they eventually arrive, how do you react?

1. You managed to get on with something while you were waiting. You are pleased and relieved to see him or her, although obviously you want to know what has happened. When they walk in you give them a big hug.

2. You are worried, fearful and anxious, can't settle to anything, and spend several hours trying to track your partner down and find out what is happening. You imagine several disasters that may have happened. When he or she walks in the door you immediately tell them how stressed out you have been and demand to know where they have been.

3. When they walk in you act cool, as if nothing has happened.

4. By the time your partner arrives you have been through all kinds of emotions and you may have mixed feelings towards them. You may not want to share your feelings. You may feel angry or rejecting, and punish your partner indirectly for their absence, or act as if you didn't mind they were late.

The four different attachment styles

1

This represents a secure attachment, and you feel you have a secure base. You generally feel safe and confident in your relationship, and this probably also reflects your own inner sense of security, which you have developed. You are not particularly jealous or possessive of each other, and can allow each other to have separate time and interests, while at the same time you intensely value the intimate connection that you have together. You are both autonomous individuals, who are able to be independent and at the same time *inter*dependent. You are able to stand back and be objective about your relationship, and to think and talk about it clearly. You can accept the fact that as an adult you still need a secure base – you don't feel the need to fight this or to deny it. Some people can be afraid that this style is too boring or safe for them. In fact it is emotionally healthy and doesn't mean you have to avoid adventure and change.

2
This represents a more anxious attachment style. You find it difficult to trust your partner completely, and things like their arriving late or their apparent interest in someone else can make you feel very insecure. You fear rejection. Your behaviour can be clingy and possessive, and you can be jealous. Sometimes you can't help this behaviour, even when it threatens to drive the other person away. Learning to feel safe and confident is a slow business, and you need your partner's understanding and support. If they also feel insecure, it can be difficult for you to offer each other the stability you both need. Sometimes it feels as if you can only get security at a price.

3
This represents an avoidant attachment style. You tell yourself to keep your distance, not to get too involved, to keep something back. You easily feel trapped or enmeshed. You don't like feeling responsible for someone else's problems. You use various tactics in the relationship to establish a safe degree of distance between you, as you can find too much intimacy and closeness to be suffocating or threatening. You may end relationships after a certain point, as you prefer to maintain the sense of being in control of your own life. You may use rejection or criticism as a tactic so that you yourself never have to feel rejected.

4
This represents an ambivalent attachment style. This means you have mixed feelings towards your partner at times, and you can blow hot or cold about the relationship. One minute you feel warm and nurturing, the next minute you want to be left alone and you can feel very critical of your partner. It is sometimes difficult for your partner to know where they stand with you. At times you

feel anxious and alone, and at other times you feel overcrowded and that you would in fact be better off alone. When people let you down, you can take it very hard. It is possible that you were expected to be independent or self-sufficient from a young age, and this has confused you somewhat so that you don't always know what you want. You know you want a close relationship, and you are capable of maintaining one, but your deeper insecurities need to be understood before you can allow yourself to be too vulnerable.

The attachment questionnaire

This is a useful way of exploring your attachment history further, and having a closer look at how it impacts on your relationships. Research shows that the ability to understand and reflect on one's emotional situation, and to explore and express your feelings about it, can make a big difference to how you cope with life. This is a powerful questionnaire that can evoke strong feelings. It is best to give yourself plenty of time to explore these questions, and to come back to them again once you have had time to think about your answers. You could go through this process with your partner when you have time to fully explore the issues involved. This will give you the opportunity to see how past and present are connected in your relationships, and what you can do to work to improve your current relationship.

1 What do you remember about your attachment style as a small child? For example, did you feel secure? Were you confident or clingy? Did you feel anxious, withdrawn or abandoned when your mother left you somewhere? Did you feel confident that she would return, and were you happy to see her again?

---

2   Who were the significant people, places or animals that you were attached to as a child? Looking back, what did these relationships mean to you?

3   Who do you think best understood you as a child? Who did you turn to when you were upset?

4   What are some words that best describe how you experienced your caregivers when you were small?

5. Did you experience the loss of any significant attachment figures? How did this affect you?

6. Did you experience any traumatic or frightening events associated with any of your significant caregivers? If so, how has this affected you? Were any of your caregivers a source of threat?

7. How did you cope and comfort yourself when things didn't go the way you wanted?

8 How did you feel when you were left at school on your first day?

9 What were your first days like at schools, colleges or in new jobs after that?

10 How do you comfort and soothe yourself now when you are upset, tired and or depressed?

11 Who do you feel relaxed and safe with now?

12 What are the things that most help you to feel loved, secure and confident in a relationship?

13 Are you afraid that you will be abandoned? Are you clingy or possessive, even if this makes it difficult for other people to be with you?

14 Do you get edgy and distant, and sometimes feel detached from the people you are close to?

15 Do you get to look after other people more than they look after you? Do you get to play a specific role in relationships?

Sexual intelligence

Sex is an opportunity for pleasure, joy, bliss, contact and meaningful connection. It offers physical relaxation and release. Sex is essential for most of us for healing, well-being, relaxation, self-expression, nurturing, ecstasy, sensuality, intimacy, oneness, release of tension and stress, and meaningful recreation. Our sense of sexual identity is essential to our sense of core identity and well-being. Sometimes we pay a high price to get the sex we need, because the need for fulfilling sex is so central to us. Nothing else gives us those feelings. Who hasn't compromised to some extent for sex – but are those compromises always worth it?

In couple relationships, sex is often the adhesive bond in a relationship, holding you together like two magnets drawn by a deep and mysterious force. Good sex brings meaning, vitality and connectedness, and most people agree that the best sex happens within an intimate and loving relationship.

Sexual intelligence is a way of thinking intelligently and creatively about sex. This is quite difficult in our present cultural context, where there is a great deal of confusion about sex and sexuality. Like religion, it is one of those areas where we receive a lot of unhelpful input, such as the association of sex with sin or guilt, seeing things in a right/wrong framework, people pretending it doesn't happen, or denying its importance. Then there is the attitude that sex is good for you and you should have as much as possible, combined with all the complex problems of sexual exploitation, abuse, sexually transmitted diseases, AIDS, debates about the morality of public figures who have affairs, and intolerance of so-called minority sexualities and sexual preferences. This is all combined with the fact that a great many people feel sexually inadequate. Our sexual energy is often repressed and distorted. Women feel self-conscious about their body image, or have difficulty getting aroused. Men get fixated on the idea of penetrative sex and performance. If you visit a sex therapist, they generally offer you advice on sexual techniques to help you relax and feel more confident, such as spending more time in affectionate touching and reducing the focus on genital sex. However, these techniques do not reach to the core of your sexual identity.

Sex is an important, creative resource to use as you choose, but it is difficult to get a clear look at what it is really all about. One's sexual energy is closely connected with one's vital life force, and needs to be respected and nurtured. Your approach to your sexuality defines who you are as an individual – gay or straight, macho or feminine, passive or dominant, conservative or adventurous. One tradition that works with sexuality in a different way is Tantra. In this tradition, our western approach to sex is seen as having severe limitations. Couples are encouraged to work with the sexual energy between them and to use it as a creative resource to build a sense of expansion and bliss. The focus is taken off achieving an orgasm, and a slower, more feminine approach is encouraged, in which you pay close attention to your feelings and to the input from all of your five senses, and remain peaceful and aware throughout the entire experience.

Explore your sexual intelligence

Think about a memorable sexual experience. What were the core components that have made it stay in your mind?

- Is sex an expression of pleasure and joy for you?
- Do you feel sexually experienced and confident?
- Do you find sex a fulfilling adventure?
- Does your sexuality express your core values?
- Have you discussed your sexual needs and expectations with your partner?
- Are you considerate of your partner's needs? Are they equal or less equal than your own?
- If your partner had sex with someone else, how would you feel? How do you feel about yourself doing this?
- Have you thought about how to keep the sexual excitement alive in your relationship?
- Are there aspects of your sexual self or fantasies you haven't yet explored? What would stop you doing this?
- Are there aspects that you find difficult or embarrassing to talk about? If so, how could you open this up?
- Do you feel happy and confident in your body and your sexuality? If not, what is the next step you could take to move forwards?
- How are spirituality and sexuality connected up for you?
- If you have experienced any form of sexual abuse, how does this still affect your sexual relationships? Are you able to discuss this with your partner?
- Have you experienced rejection or prejudice because of your sexual orientation? How has this affected your relationship to your own sexuality?
- What would your dream, ideal sexual experience be like?

conclusion: hope

With hope we can accomplish great things.

Consider your life at this moment. Rate yourself on these questions using the following scale:

A = all of the time;
B = most of the time;
C = a lot of the time;
D = some of the time;
E = a bit of the time.

1. I am actively expressing my chosen values.
2. Although I may not always be able to explain why, I feel hopeful and optimistic.
3. I am learning, growing and developing as a person.
4. I am energetically pursuing my chosen goals.
5. I see myself as being successful and effective.
6. I know I can tackle the problems I am facing right now.
7. I feel my past experience has given me wisdom for the future.
8. I know if I persist, I will eventually reach my goals.
9. I see and express my own potential for happiness and creativity.
10. My relationships are a source of comfort, nurture and inspiration.
11. I reflect on myself, and express my values and feelings.

By daring to dream and daring to live by our most dearly held, exciting and empowering personal values, we can work together in the spirit of hope.

Hope is a fantastic resource of the human spirit, easily stifled by the dead weight of cynicism and destructiveness, but which springs anew if given space to breathe and grow.

May your hope and your values grow wings, soar high, and find the depth and breadth of a positive, freely chosen, hopeful attitude to your own and our collective lives.

Notes, References and Further Reading

Chapter 1
The links between self-esteem, positive feelings about oneself and one's world and better results in life have been extensively documented. See, just as one example, Isen, A., 'The Facilitating Influence of Positive Affect on Social Behaviour and Cognitive Processes', in C.R. Snyder and S.J. Lopez (eds) (2002), *Handbook of Positive Psychology*, Oxford University Press, New York.

Chapter 2
Much work in the field of positive psychology has focused on values – beginning with Maslow, A.H. (1970), *Motivation and Personality*, Harper and Row, New York.

Values can be defined as fundamentally moral, accepted by choice, and a code to guide one's choices and fulfil one's needs. No two people can hold identical values.

Victor Frankl, who was incarcerated in a concentration camp, and survived to write about how some people survived and others did not, emphasised that we need a sense of meaning to survive difficult experiences. Values are the main form of meaning. However, we don't nowadays have any social consensus about values, and the onus is now on us as individuals to define these for ourselves, and find ways in which we can experience and fulfil them. Frankl, V.E. (1976), *Man's Search for Meaning*, Pocket Books, New York (original work published 1959).

This is also linked to the ability to set and fulfil specific value-driven goals for oneself; see, for example:

Snyder, C.R. (1994), *The Psychology of Hope: You Can Get There from Here*, Free Press, New York.

McDermott, H.D. & Snyder, C.R. (2000), *The Great Big Book of Hope: Help Your Children Achieve Their Dreams*, New Harbinger Press, Oakland, CA.

Chapter 3
New and current positive psychology approaches to stress and stress management are much more optimistic and less fatalistic than in the past. They show how versatile and adaptive many people can be in

response to life stressors. They grow stronger, and acquire a greater sense of meaning and efficacy as a result. See, for example:

Seligman, M.E.P. (1998), *Learned Optimism: How to Change Your Mind and Your Life*, Pocket Books, New York.

Chapter 4

There are numerous techniques, books and therapies available on psychotherapeutic approaches to working with the past. However, a central question seems to be the choice between what constitutes unhealthy self-preoccupation, self-indulgence and self-pity, and what constitutes denial, avoidance and general lack of emotional competence or awareness. The general consensus seems to be that experience must be fully conscious and understood before one can bounce back.

For a complete list of the official diagnostic criteria for Post Traumatic Stress Disorder (PTSD), as well as depression and any other mental health issues, see American Psychiatric Association (1994), *Diagnostic and Statistical Manual of Mental Disorders*, 4th edn, Washington DC.

Sigmund Freud's seminal paper of 1917, 'Mourning and Melancholia', still makes fascinating reading. You can find it in *Standard Edition of the Complete Psychological Works of Sigmund Freud*, Vol. 14, Hogarth Press, London. The 1909 quotation from Freud is taken from 'Analysis of a Phobia in a Five-Year-Old Boy', *Standard Edition*, Vol. 10.

Winnicott, D. (1971), *Playing and Reality*, Penguin, London, is another classic text that vividly describes how the child's evolving relationship with the mother lays the foundation for creativity and health.

Chapter 5

Happiness and creativity research are now getting much more attention than ever before. See, for example, the World Database of Happiness website at Erasmus University, Rotterdam at http://www.eur.nl.fsw/research/happiness

Some suggestions for the dimensions of well-being are taken from the research quoted in Keyes, C.L.M. & Lopez, S.J., 'Toward a Science of Mental Health: Positive Directions in Diagnosis and Interventions', in C.R. Snyder & S.J. Lopez (eds) (2002), *Handbook of Positive Psychology*, Oxford University Press, New York.

See also:

Csikszentmihalyi, M. (1991), *Flow: The Psychology of Optimal Experience*, Harper Perennial, New York.

– (1996), *Creativity*, Harper Collins, New York.

– (2000), *Beyond Boredom and Anxiety*, Jossey-Bass, San Francisco (original book published 1975).

Chapter 6

The introductory quote is from Myers, D.G. (1992), *The Pursuit of Happiness: Who Is Happy and Why*, William Morrow, New York.

See also:

Beck, A. (1988), *Love is Never Enough*, Harper & Row, New York.

Gottman, J. (1995), *Why Marriages Succeed and Fail*, Fireside, New York. This researcher carried out some fascinating studies using an apartment-laboratory to observe the communication behaviour of couples.

Schwartz, P. (1994), *Peer Marriage*, Free Press, New York. This writer introduced the idea that successful modern marriages have changed substantially and now rely a great deal more on friendship qualities.

Tannen, D. (1990), *You Just Don't Understand: Women and Men in Conversation*, Morrow, New York. While this book has been frequently quoted, Tannen's insights into the differences between men's and women's expectations in a conversation still make illuminating reading.

Welwood, J. (1990), *Journey of the Heart: The Path to Deeper Fulfilment in Relationships*, Harper Collins, New York. This is a readable book on the more spiritual dimensions of relationship, as is:

Welwood, J. (ed.) (1985), *Challenge of the Heart: Love, Sex and Intimacy in Changing Times*, Shambhala, Boston, which is a compilation of essays by a wide range of writers.

An enjoyable introduction to personality types based on the Myers-Briggs Type Indicator, which includes introversion and extroversion as one of four different personality scales, making up sixteen different personality types, can be found in, for example, Kroeger, O. & Thuesen, J.M. (1988), *Type Talk: The 16 Personality Types that Determine How We Live, Love and Work*, Bantam Doubleday, New York.

A general introduction to attachment theory can be found in Holmes, J. (1993), *John Bowlby and Attachment Theory*, Routledge, London.